Big & Small Treasures of the Heart and Soul

Tany V.

Dedication

In memory of my daughter Jammie Lynn, for all the love she gave her family and friends and never asked for anything in return. A beautiful soul who left us too soon. Our lives will never be the same. You will always be in our hearts and will never be forgotten!

Acknowledgment

First and foremost, I would like to thank the Lord for his eternal guidance and for showering me with His blessing throughout my life. Alleluia!

I also want to express my deepest appreciation to the entire staff of Delta Ghostwriting, and especially Alan Hill, my Project Manager, for his immense contribution—likewise, the realization of my new book Big & Small Treasures of the Heart and Soul. I surely couldn't have undertaken this journey without his expertise and unparalleled advice in creating the birth of my dream using all the resources required to make the book project unforgettable.

I am looking forward to broadening my creativity and honoring all my followers' interests.

May the Almighty bless us all.

About the Author

I was born in Havana, Cuba, and raised in Caracas, Venezuela. After my graduation, I moved to Miami, Florida, as I began my songwriting career. Blessed by the gift of music and afterward, my interest in writing poetry developed, enhancing a whole new world of possibilities.

My first book, *Treasures of the Heart*, was published in 2019, around the same time COVID-19 began. Being a first-time author, it was quite difficult to promote as we were all enduring challenging times. Foremost, my second book, *Treasures of the Soul: with a Spanish Flare*, has received a promotional offer from the Spotlight Network with Logan Crawford Anchor, Reporter.

Throughout my songwriting and singing career, I have received many awards. Therefore, I am connecting with my followers once again as an author of my new book, *Big & Small Treasures of the Heart and Soul*.

I hope this book becomes a special and rewarding read. It is all about the feeling of the heart and the pure inspiration of the soul. I like to author poems filled with charismatic enchantment, a little fantasy, and undeniable adventure. A magical, unique vision that provides a perfect ingredient. It fulfills my life with true purpose.

I have received awards from Poetry Nation, Nallen and Scryptor, Brilliant Literary Books, Eber & Wein, and others. My passion and devotion to the arts are a flame that lives inside me with every passing day.

The birth of my dream involves romance, fiction, thrillers, fairy tales, children's poems, storytelling of real-life family stories, and a lot of love and devotion.

I very much want to delight and entertain readers of all genres; that is why my book holds a special, unique style that can captivate any reader.

I'm looking forward to a journey of memorable times and accomplishments.

Preface

This book grew in a secret place inside my heart. I have thought of every feasible way to enhance it with the most detailed writing I could think of. It is all about a "writer's brain."

Making every poem and story like it has really happened! Although, some poems are true passages of my life.

A "field of dreams" I wanted to share with all of those who love a bit of romance, fantasy, inspiration, storytelling, and so much more.

Breathtaking feelings and a little pizazz toward the birth of my creation.

Having the privilege to present my humble work to all my followers is an amazing opportunity.

I wanted to write a simple but entertaining read to delight every genre.

With patience, dedication, and the ambition to compile an array of marvelous stories that are going to touch your spirit, heart, and soul.

I would like to introduce *Big and Small Treasures of the Heart and Soul*. I hope that it will captivate everyone's passion.

Venturing into the world of literature has, without a doubt, exceeded my expectations toward a "remarkable and exceptional journey."

Contents

Children

A Child's Imagination

I want to be an eagle so I can fly and see the world.

I want to be a mouse to squeeze through everywhere.

I want to be a tiger so I can growl and cautiously hunt.

Although, I want to be a bull so I can fight and be the champ.

I want to be a beaver and learn how to build.

I want to be a horse to gallop straight down the hill.

I want to be a chameleon so I can easily transform.

But I would rather be a whale traveling the ocean floors.

I want to be a deer and timidly hide.

I want to be a cat to land on your lap.

I want to be a dog and just feel your loving touch.

Though, I really want to be a seagull to soar in the skies above.

I want to be a bee so I can honey you around.

I want to be a bear to hug you to the ground.

I want to be a hen and lay an egg for you.

Nevertheless, I want to be a rooster and cock-a-doodle-doo.

I want to be a butterfly and thus flutter into your heart.

I want to be a spider to web myself on and on.

I want to be a fish so I can swim and wave goodbye.

However, I really want to be a firefly to light your way at night.

I want to be a dog.

Bow wow, bow wow, bow wow!

I want to be a duck.

Quack, quack, quack!

I want to be a cow.

Moo, moo, moo!

I want to be a cat.

Meow, meow, meow!

A child's imagination is packed with inspiration and motivation.

"No matter what! Always remember to be yourself."

A Princess Story

Being a princess requires strict finesse.
Living in a palace with guards at your doorstep.
Fly on a magic carpet ride
through clouds of "dreams and love."
A princess has a lot of responsibilities to follow.
Be proper, educated, and well-refined.
Listen and obey the rules that dictate the throne.
Therefore, working toward the goal
of becoming queen and ruler of the land.
Twinkling stars will shower down.
Then, find a prince from the Royal family.
He will have to be the perfect one.
Regardless, my marriage is already agreed-upon.
I must get used to the idea of falling in love
with someone I have never met before.
The reason I'll become a queen, sadly, relied entirely
on the passing of "King George VI," my father "Hail to the King!"
Which made me heir to the throne.
"A Royal ceremony will take place at my Coronation."
Receiving upon my head the Crown "Symbol of Regal Authority."
So, here I am ready for the commitment of becoming a queen.

"But most of all, a fair human being, which is the most difficult
of all tasks."
A life of a queen is based on proper measures
for the sake and stable growth of the throne!

Campesina

Long ago, in a distant place, a precious girl

by the name of Campesina was born.

She learned to talk to the animals,

an unbelievable true animal whisperer.

Residents would visit her from the nearby communities and even

faraway towns.

Asking for her help concerning the welfare of their pets.

Her impressive intuition could figure out if the animal

was anxious, nervous, or plainly ill.

She would look the animal straight in their eyes

as she knew right away what was wrong and how to fix the problem.

The President's pet became extremely ill, but despite

all the expensive vet visits, the poor little dog wasn't

getting any better.

He would tremble and stop eating for no obvious reason.

Raising all kinds of red flags, the pet seemed in distress all the time.

Their spoiled little Yorkie by the name of Jewels needed help!

So, they called Campesina for her ability.

Two agents went to Campesina's house to pick her up.

Campesina was a bit confused.

Why would the President of the United States

put any kind of trust in a simple country girl like me?

Summoned by the President, she agreed to go to the White House.

Once she got there, everyone greeted her as she walked across the

main entrance;

guarded heavily by the President's bodyguards.

When she got to the room, she unpacked being tired from the trip.

She ate a snack and fell asleep right away.

The next morning, after having the most amazing breakfast,

she asked to see Jewels. He was a puny little thing, and

she began petting his head.

Jewels' condition had been going on for a while, but no one

could really tell why!

After about ten minutes, he began showing signs of stress.

Poor Jewels was in a lot of pain and discomfort.

She then looked into his eyes and concluded he was

lacking self-control.

An illness of the nervous system was making him tremble.

She also realized he had a small lump on his head.

Although it did not appear to be swollen, it was tender to the touch.

The President came down to greet and make acquaintances

with Campesina.

She told the President that Jewels needed a special multivitamin

and prebiotics for his treatment.

As for the lump on his head, she advised a special oil with

vitamins and menthol would

take care of making it disappear.

The President asked Campesina how long it would take for the

treatment to work.

Do not worry, Mr. President, it will work since I spoke to Jewels,

and he explained

everything he was feeling. Jewels will be fine in no time.

After two weeks, Jewels was himself again.

The President could not believe it.

Jewels were not trembling anymore

or feeling any pain.

Being so happy with the outcome, he sent Campesina a beautiful

gift and an award

for her exceptional talent,

A truly "Miraculous Animal Whisperer."

Doggy in the Window

I have always been in love with the doggy in the window.

What a charming notion that has faded through the years.

Always wanting to jump up, wagging his tail non-stop.

He wants to let you know that he is ready to go home.

He will play a circus clown to win you all around.

Whimpering to change your mind as you hold him in your arms.

With those big teary eyes that really make you want to cry.

Do not worry, little fellow, you will soon be smitten with

lots of warmth.

Someone to change your world to be filled with love.

Keep you safe always and give you lots of hugs!

I know you will be a friendly one.

"Your purpose in life will be complete."

Just because you wished upon a star

and found a warm loving heart.

You will grow to be a strong, good old pup, a faithful dog for

years to come.

Through it all, you will be remembered!

"As the Doggy in the Window we all grew to love."

For the Children

Peace on earth for the children of the world.
Let us fight for their salvation!
Love and bless the children of the world.
Let them grow through generations.
Look through the eyes of the future.
Look through the eyes of the world.
Believe in the voices of the children; they are the perfect
miracle of love.
Look at the smiles on their faces and the joy when a
child is born.
They own the gift of beauty, "what the world is so hungry for!"
Caring for and protecting the children
keeps them safe every day.
They will be the light of tomorrow;
hold them tight in your arms and pray.
Look through the eyes of the innocent;
their tenderness will touch your heart.
They depend on our protection
as they wait at home with open arms.
Look through the eyes of the universe.
Wake up to a changed and better place,
safe from harm and awful violence.

Besides, their dreams will never end.

Love and care for the children; the wind will silence their pain.

"May the power of goodness win over evil!"

Praying for the world to become "Love and Peace" once again.

(Too much violence is hurting our children).

Hello Critters

Over the prairie next to the hill.

On top of the mountain where the boughs of the Juniper grow.

High flies the Sunbird over the bridge

in the valley of splendor surrounded by peace.

Coins in the fountain, frogs in the pond.

Sunflowers blooming, squirrels gliding for fun.

Butterflies dancing, dragonflies begin to hide.

Rivers flow gently in the rhythm of life.

The cow flew over the moon; the clock strikes noon.

Bunny's hopping away; cats ready to play.

Bees buzz for honey; bears dig for sweets.

Chicks looking for pellets pecking the ground they feed.

Foxes drench from the rain; chipmunks buried in the dirt.

Deer running for cover; reindeer share their domain.

Kittens meow, hungry and cold, looking for refuge and warmth.

Cause the trap caught the mouse and the cheese rolled down.

The tiny green turtle crawled out of the shell.

The spider wiggled the web, but the piggy ate instead.

Water in the kettle helps quench the nettle.

Nevertheless, birds are singing, and pups are wiggling their tails.

Koi swims downstream, eating coral and giant beans.

The barn houses horses, goats, and sheep.

But outside, the little birds are chirping and spreading the news

of every critter around our home,

which has an adventure to tell, in a nutshell.

Little Girl and Precious Angel

Silent words fearfully awaiting.

When I saw her eyes, I knew she was awakened.

Then, I held her little hands and, in my arms, embraced her.

The first word I heard you say

I remember when it was just like yesterday.

You're mommy's little girl and daddy's precious angel.

Wearing hats and pearls dancing on the table.

Even though we know this time won't last forever.

But in our eyes, you will always be

our little girl and precious angel.

One day, you'll become a bride. "Wow! Graceful butterfly."

From my life, you will fly away, but in my soulfulness,

you will remain.

I will treasure every kiss goodnight

instigating in our little fights.

You'll be part of me even if I am gone.

Our treasured memories will be written in pure gold.

"You are the star that illuminates our lives forever."

Because you will always be

my little girl and daddy's precious angel.

Little Kid's Story

One early morning, I got out of bed
many questions are stuck in my head.
I wonder if the moth that landed on my pillow
wanted to sleep and be safe from other critters?
I wonder if the beetles' making noises against the window
found something good to eat?
I wonder if the raccoon scratching the rooftop
somehow managed a way in?
I wonder if the spider lurking in the ceiling webbing all night
while preying on the weak?
I wonder if the mouse chewing on the wall
finally found food for his family?
I wonder if the frogs croaking around found water to quench
their necessity?
I wonder if my prayer was finally answered
to always have God's light shining over me?

My Pony

Riding on top of my pony, gentle and cute as can be.
Trotting along up the mountain down to the pond, racing free!
I braid his hair with twine and tassels
looking good wherever he goes.
Through fields of wondrous poppy flowers.
He is quick to gallop, looking tall.
I love to listen to the sounds.
"Clip-clop or clip pity-clop on the road."
He is my playful little pony.
"The best friend I have ever known."

Princess

Once there was a princess, her name was Sarahbella.

She loved to wear sparkling gowns and glitter in her hair.

Her crown would shine so ever bright with

ruby and diamond stones.

However, she loved her friends so much with every single

caring thought.

They would play board games and dress their dolls too.

Sing a song or even run through the castle's empty rooms.

"The king and queen were immensely proud

of the sweetness in her heart."

They taught their little princes to be always good and kind.

Adored by her Kingdom, where everyone bowed their heads.

"The knights knelt by her side and kissed her hand instead."

Until her fateful day when she becomes a mighty queen.

Courageous and brave to reign over the land genuinely.

"All will rejoice with happiness

and lift their swords to the very end!"

Hail to the Queen! My friends, Hail to the Queen!

The Horse

Run! Run! With the wind.

Like a horse through green pastures.

"Where rainbows form."

Wild and spirited, running free!

"In the field of dreams glowing like a star."

Changing through the seasons every year.

With each passing day, you become strong and bright.

As your strength will be the reigns,

which controls the subtle commands of the horse.

The Lamb & the Yellow Daffodils

How precious the lamb plays

with yellow daffodils beside her where she lays.

Her white wool tangled up in the wind and

her pretty face brightens the morning breeze.

How cute she often grins.

"From one place to the other as she spins."

Waiting for the daffodils to grow out from the South.

A persistent scent they carry about.

The soft petals taste so unique.

The lamb knows which ones to pick.

Sometimes, she wears them on top of her coat and

even rolls on them when the petals float.

"Lambs and daffodils go together."

Funny how they know exactly where they grow

outstandingly clever.

"To catch a glance or a little snack from the gifts of the daffodils."

The Story of Willie the Kid

He adventured for days in a pirate ship

set out to find treasures deep in the sea.

"Strong as an ox, always ready to succeed."

One day, he found an old treasure map.

It was concealed in the basement inside a wooden box.

So, he searched night and day to find it at last!

He was sure the jewels were hidden away but not far.

In dark caves deep down at the bottom of the sea.

"Where treasures are covered by sand and coral reefs."

He dove from the ship, swimming like a fish then

followed the marks and began the treasure hunt

for days, even weeks.

Willie the Kid ventured, following the stars.

He was afraid of nothing, and his strength was amazingly sharp.

He would not give up until the jewels were safely in his hands.

He remembered legends of mermaid keepers of the riddles and

hoards ready to be acquired.

Willie got a glimpse of the cave where the treasure secretly hid.

But when he went inside, he only found traces of empty lids.

He could not believe how unlucky he felt.

However, someone had beaten him to the entire wealth.

He kept on searching with only hope in his heart.

"If it is not this one, many more are still up for grabs."

Sinking ships stay buried deep in the depths of our dreams.

Treasures that belong to the furious and hungry sea.

Buried and waiting to be discovered, and who better than

Willie the kid?

The most fearless treasure hunter that ever lived!

Where Would I Fly?

"When I was young, I wanted to fly."
I don't know where, but somewhere high.
Just like birds flopping their wings
flying forever against the wind.
Climbing the top of every rooftop
nothing stands in their way.
Regardless, I wonder where I would go.
"Frankly, I really don't seem to know."
Maybe where dreams really come true.
Where marigolds begin to bloom.
Somewhere, anywhere, I really don't know!
Most of all, if I ever got the chance to fly,
I would wonder with every wish in mind.
"Living a bewildering and astonishing life."

Family

Beloved Sister

Growing up! I remembered building 'castles' in the sand.

We hid things from each other, and our bond grew forever strong.

We made up names for our boyfriends,

but sometimes, we disagreed.

We share dreams and hopes together;

you took my 'heart' and left the 'key.'

Your soul was sick and tired and had no strength to fight anymore;

therefore, the Lord understood your struggles

as he carried you back home.

I tried to send you a message as a sign that I am all right.

"It is so beautiful here in Heaven."

"I am finally free and fine."

I know you are sitting in Heaven watching over me.

I miss every moment of every day as you guard my every sleep.

Do not worry about me, sister, I closely hold our memories.

I still hear your special laughter deep inside of me.

You were taken by the wings of angels.

However, in my heart, you will always stay.

I feel your presence in every whisper, like a bird singing in the rain

"You will always and forever be."

My "treasured friend," my "loving sis,"

the "bravest!" that lives inside of me!

Broken Love

Life can change at any time, and it did for me

on an unexpected September night.

Betrayed by a daughter who I held dearly in my heart.

Teardrops falling down my face,

but sadness gushing through my veins.

When will this sorrow end?

When will peace be regained?

Abrogating bad intentions growing in the depth of

My broken love.

Placing my total trust in her, not knowing good intentions

were vague.

Tearing a hole in my heart so deep it almost bled.

But she only found chuckling joy at my aching pain.

Feeling miserable and confused through life's turning points.

Fighting these incomprehensible feelings, I can't ever let go.

However, my "soul demands empathy and forgiveness."

as crewel emotions hit hard through the center of my soul.

Feeling like a ragged doll dragged in the mud.

Screaming! For help, besides, no one listened.

Keeping myself composure; however, nowhere to go!

Realizing nothing else mattered but the devotion

I felt for someone that did not deserve my love.

Nevertheless, hindered and devastated by her

evilness destroyed hope in myself.

Listening to wrongful influences which turn out of control.

Ripping apart a special bond, moreover,

grew like a "lily flower for so long."

Do not make excuses for the mistake you have made.

Faults never fall far, only hide beneath the pain.

It takes a brave moment to understand you were wrong.

Unfortunately, life throws tough chapters to make us strong!

"Blood is thicker than water." Why would you sell your heart to

devilish roads?

Instead of choosing honest love as your only resource.

Stop! Stabbing the heart, hiding feelings you own.

Let your true gut be your guide; otherwise create positive vibes.

Believing in yourself is the key to your success.

The best way is to change the way you act.

"By building compassion in your heart."

Farewell

Bells are ringing at the entrance of a lifeless body
inside a wooden coffin.
My cold flesh and bones resting on a white satin cushion.
A crowd of family members and friends find themselves,
weeping through hours of pain, grief, and sorrow.
"Don't they know death is just a transition to another
sphere of consciousness?"
Although, in my perpetual dream state, I looked
peacefully resting.
Perhaps, waiting for relatives to guide me across
my new destination.
Lips frozen in time, but a smile remained.
My eyes closed forever but appeared placid.
My hands hovered over a crucifix covered in white roses
strongly appropriate for the occasion.
As the moment arrived with the last goodbye,
tears embellish the casket, lowering itself onto the ground.
The wind began whistling sounds of music and
soft murmurs touched everyone present.
No more bodily functions, only a soul ready
to escape to a different place.
At once, I was flying into and out of a dark narrow corridor

a new beginning was awaiting at last!

a new beginning was awaiting at last!
However, I felt being pulled back and forth
by a raging black storm.
I was screaming in agonizing pain as I felt
a hot wave melting through me.
Panic and terror struck like a ravaging violent frenzy.
"Oh! God, please help me," something is trying to snatch
me away!
"My call was answered, and sprinkles of golden rain showered
down on me."
Despite my struggles, a light of hope holds onto my hands.
It was my mother's hands which guided me
to cross over the "Stairway to Heaven."

Final Wishes

I have never really given a thought as to when I am going to go.

Occasionally, I have a gut feeling it is not going to be unpleasant at all.

Simply a welcoming sigh of relief when the time comes around.

"Knowing I have fulfilled my purpose and dreams, that is all I care about."

"Nothing left to pledge, all written clearly step-by-step."

Leaving a lengthy list of instructions to evade quarrels instead.

Keeping in mind the cat and dog for their amazing love they never hesitate to give.

But I do not know who will deliver my last and concluding list.

From the pretenders who abandoned me and took another road.

Obviously, all who gripped my last wishes are included here within, even the greediest who never cared for anything.

I do not judge since that is what the Lord says.

Therefore, I am thinking of everyone, and that is my final request.

I was taught to believe someone will care until the end.

"As when I am gone, I am all prepared to take another stairway."

I only know good memories will abide in my heart forever.

Remembering those who never left me stranded whatsoever!

Gone But Not Forgotten

Do not cry on my deathbed.

It is simply the doorway to a new beginning.

Nonetheless, it is hard to say farewell.

"I will never forget the creation of my life."

Listen to the bells tolling to the rhythm of my last heartbeat.

I needed to slow down the pace of having to please everyone else

but myself.

However, no matter how much I tried, it was not enough.

Haven't I given my all? What else can I bring to the table?

Make everyone happy, I just do not know.

At times I felt very depressed, like taking my last breath.

I had everyone around me, even though I felt entirely alone.

Do they know how sad I was?

How many times I've cried myself to sleep?

Holding on to my broken heart and staring at my loneliness.

Saddened from deprived attention,

needing a shoulder to rest on.

Silently shedding tears through the night.

Where were you when my life was slipping away

from my hands?

When my time was running out, tell me, where were you?

Someday, when it all ends, think of me alive.

Remember every detail, every memory,
every moment and hold on to my story in your heart.
"My love will never cease to exist."
Like a brushfire, it will linger in every place and
every reminiscence.

Happy Dad's Day

Today is Father's Day.

I wish you all the best.

For everything you have done and do.

I've made this special day for you!

I know it is not an easy task but still

you never seem to pause.

Your time, protection, and love are a blessing from above.

I hope you know I am glad to have you as my dad.

I knew you were that special man with a big, amazing heart!

Attentive to my every need, a trusting father who I love indeed.

My refuge and rock who shared his time to play and talk.

Rest assured, I am forever proud

for all the fun times and sad ones, too, you cared about.

In spite our sweet relationship

"I pray God will keep you safe for me."

When I am all grown up, I will cherish the love

and sacrifices you did not hesitate to make.

"You are now and will always be my greatest loving dad!"

Jammie Lynn

Walking down the pathway of my past.

I remembered stories stored in my mind.

One I've never forgotten!

It's a funny one that left an impression for years to come.

Becoming a young bride and mother at the same time

was an overwhelming effort.

Nonetheless, it helped me grow and mature swiftly.

As she began calling me mommy, it hit my heart

like a freight train!

Couldn't believe I was part of her plan.

A mere three-year-old walked into my life.

With shiny green eyes, perfect red apple-shaped face,

rosy cheeks, and a smile; "that would wake up the world."

As she held my hand, we moved slowly to the pond.

She had bird food saved up in her red plastic cup.

A duck approached unexpectedly.

Immediately, she became startled because he wanted food too.

With a silly grin, she replied in her babbling baby talk.

"Goo Gaga" plus the 'F' word, crazy duck!

We all laughed hysterically; and without any doubt

"It became a family joke."

Therefore, dad seemed a bit embarrassed by her

inappropriate words.

Truthfulness is a gift only small children own.

As she grew older, I always saw myself in her.

She was giving, warm, loving, and the best sister anyone could

"dream of."

My first baby girl is my friend now and my "confidant."

Our love couldn't be measured,

it grows every day like trees in the fields.

She will always be my special first baby girl.

Her love was the most precious gift blessed by

"The Power of Love."

Now she has traveled to another place.

She's here but not near; only good memories are still palpable.

As in her journey she will be a shining star

looking over us in the great distance.

Flying free from her terrible disease, falling in the arms of Jesus

"Resting in Peace."

Don't ever forget we hold you close in our thoughts and dreams.

"Farewell, my beloved daughter,

we are missing you tremendously."

(In memory of my daughter Jammie Lynn.)

My Broken-Hearted Granddaughter

Watching my first grandchild's birth was the most

gratifying experience of my life!

Such a beautiful moment holding her tight

in my arms, gently humming a lullaby.

Little bundle of joy; looking at her made me cry.

Through the years, I watched her grow,

blowing candles on her birthday, seeing her glow.

Learning as much as she could was a must,

when schoolwork came along.

We would read together, play, and have fun!

All and all, misery can strike any home

and did for sure on a gloomy eerie dawn.

Looking through the corner of her eyes and afraid of the night.

As she built strength to battle her emotions inside.

A terrifying feeling was a step away, which

tore a hole in her heart with no escape but sobbing pain.

Drowning in confusion despite trying to forget.

Although face-to-face, with abuse and vivid scars

buried in the dirt.

Why was she forced to endure cruelty along the way?

I saw anger and rage running through her veins.

Like stumbling on the same stone with nothing to gain.

Stalked by this nightmare in her sleepless state.

Looking for answers to questions she could not understand.

Feeling guilty about herself and getting

hurt by the trusted hand.

Helpless body tossed like a used garment, ugly and ashamed.

It is so hard putting herself on the right track of

forgetting the past.

Placing Band-Aid on scars that do not want to heal,

no matter what!

Protect her somehow from the jaws of destiny and fate.

Living in fantasy is not enough

and bad dreams are overwhelming.

Only my love I could give,

but she was holding on to a broken heart instead.

Finally came graduation, and I was so happy and proud.

Ready to face new challenges and opportunities in her life.

Sorting out priorities for her new lifestyle.

It all fit like a glove; the light eventually shined on her side.

She is a grown-up woman now with different aspirations.

Long roads ahead with assertiveness and determination.

We all experience sad moments and turmoil through time.

After many years, in some way,

she found closure and put her anger aside.

No matter what happened, she tried to heal her broken heart.

One day in spring, she delivered a son.

For sure the happiest person I had ever known.

Carried him for hours, afraid to let him go

for his presence relieved anxiety tucked away in her soul.

She felt complete once more, thanking God for the gift she holds.

Drying her teary eyes open wounds, I cannot ever let go.

My broken-hearted little girl, how could I've saved you so?

But you have been given a second chance to hold on to

your precious love.

That is a blessing from the above!

"Always to be thankful for."

My Childhood Dreams

Waking up every morning with millions of ideas in my head.

Doing my chores makes me bored, something I always dread.

Never a tedious moment, but excitement follows me.

Wishes will always come true if you honestly believe.

I want to become a movie star or a singer with lots of fans.

A doctor or a lawyer year of study which never ends.

Nothing stands in the way of a young mind ready to expand,

with all kinds of adventures and imagination ready to land.

Reinforced every idea collected like a strong gust of wind.

Everything looks bright and beautiful; no worries at all.

"It is a wonderful feeling you develop as you grow."

Free-spirited young child with an open future to roam.

"All is possible when your heart is on the go."

No matter if life brings struggles, your power conquers along.

Besides, all that stays is my wishful list of fantastic dreams

to uphold.

Finally, become someone important

and leave your name printed in bold.

"It is my dream to set aside a legacy to be read

when hope is lost."

Stories and poems inspired by passion

which means the world as I know.

I have published books of romance, fantasy,

even science fiction, and quotes.

Also, children's stories are overflowing with emotions

that will linger on and on.

Composed songs of unforgettable meaning

which I carry deep in my soul.

"Behold the future of childhood dreams.

That one day will be shared;

with all those around the world that dream and fall in love."

My Grandkids and Great Grandkids

What precious gifts received from life!

What wondrous memories of each single one!

"Family is the essence of riches anyone could ever have."

With every child born, a new beginning which brings joy.

Never a tedious moment, with the passing of the years.

Receiving every morning a special kiss

which you hold forever through the years.

Going out to places and enjoying so much quality time.

Spending all day with grandkids is the most remarkable and greatly

grandly.

"It is priceless to learn how much they grow with every year of

their lives."

How drastically they change with each birthday passing by.

I remember when they were small, and I sang them cradle songs.

In my memoir book, I keep track of every event

and mind you, I have a lot.

Baptisms, Communions, Birthdays, Christmas, Weddings,

and so much more!

Always taking part in every important and treasured moment

I hold.

"Nothing can be more special than what you leave behind."

Years not to be forgotten but kept alive in the rhythm of life.

My Passion for Baking

It began when I was a young girl in the care of my grandparents.

My 'Grandmother,' being a great baker, began teaching me the art of baking.

"Nothing tasted better than a homemade cake, bread, pie, muffin, or pastry in general."

My favorite thing to do was build the decoration and watch the result!

Every sugar flower or frosting which embellished the beauty and mouth-watering desire to grab a single piece was Heaven sent!

"I remember spending hours with Grandma in the kitchen."

She would teach me the magic of playing with the dough, stretching it, forming the texture, caressing every inch, and making sure it was perfect!

"I very much miss her guidance."

Especially the way she taught me with immense patience.

I sometimes see myself baking in the kitchen with her by my side.

"However, she was a perfectionist. I really thank her from my heart for all her devoted time."

Grandma shared her knowledge and creativity of the most beautiful and appetizing cakes.

"That is one of the most important gifts we can receive from our elders."

The legacy they leave behind for future generations.

Of course, I still love to bake the ones with strawberries, cherries, and chocolate truffles.

Thank you, Granny, for the unforgettable time.

Thank You, Mom

With every word and every cuddle,
I felt your warmth and tenderness.
You cradle me through the night
as you kept a watchful, loving eye.
You heard my every little cry;
how I stretched and moved around
Touching my hands and cute little toes
wrapped me in a blanket to keep me warm.
Restless and tiresome, your day begins.
Patiently feeding and changing me constantly.
Being a mommy requires lots of sacrifices:
A lifetime commitment that goes forever and never-ending.
But you poured out your loving heart
through every hard stage of my life.
Your warmth and love were
the best blessings I could ever have.
Therefore, I hope one day I will care for you
with the same boundless love.
Your incredible care grew deep in my heart
helped me succeed for years to come.
Even when I failed, your open arms
were always there to hold me tight.

For everything you have ever done,

I am proud to be your child.

As one day, I will become a parent too.

"I pray to the Lord I will be as perfect as you."

I thank you for being my mom.

The Baby

The baby is here!

I know I'll sing and cheer.

"Making sure everything is clean and clear."

A toy car that he can steer, and

will brighten his atmosphere.

Hoping he doesn't have his father's ears. Ha! Ha! Ha!

We celebrate with wine and root beer.

Sometimes, shedding a little tear.

"But nothing is more important, my dear,

than a healthy baby blessed by God

to hold and love throughout the years."

Fantasy

Birthday Wish

A falling star appeared in the night.
A wish was made,
which touched the heart.
A dream came true
in the wings of time.
Beloved; forever
in the "bliss of light."

Dragon Slayer

By the wrath of a dragon,

the castle burns in the crossfire.

A Dragon Slayer and knights

fight to regain control of the battle.

Together, joining forces to kill the dragon.

Then finally, overpower him with special

swords made of steel and onyx stones.

Triumph at last!

Simultaneously saving the people of the town and the castle.

The Empire rises tall in heroic voices

which are heard on the distant shore.

Long live the Dragon Slayer!

Long live his courage!

Once Upon a Dream

Once upon a time, I wished for a dream to come true.

Confident, I rested by the roots of an ageless Oak tree.

As I fell into a profound sleep,

I could see myself all covered in roses.

But in my hands rested a book of my life story.

I suddenly opened my eyes, a handsome

prince knelt by my side.

He kissed my lips and read the book along the faded lines.

Then, he just laid beside me in a dream, lost for all times.

When I think of him, it all becomes so clear.

Beside a wishing well a treasure box appeared.

riding a gentle Pegasus covered in silk and gold.

Bewitched by his enchantment where crystal rain falls.

As I traveled through the clouds, envisioning a dragon.

Reaching the castle walls, the knights were prepared for battle.

I was looking for the prince, but he was nowhere to be found.

Therefore, I continued my journey flying through the stars.

"On my once upon a time."

Walking deep in the forest, I met the prince once again.

On his knees, he promised to love me forever, Amen.

He held me close and tenderly as he whispered in my ear.

Our love will never be forgotten as the April snow, as the first morning of spring, as a mesmerizing dream.

"Of once upon a time."

Then, he took the book and read it through

along the faded lines of mystical lakes,

wishing wells, and Unicorns everywhere!

"Upon a dream."

The Magic Hat

One afternoon in early spring, an elderly lady sat on her swing.

Very well dressed in vintage green, wearing her favorite ring.

She wanted to buy a hat or two,

so she walked down the street to the mall.

Going inside an antique store, she saw beautiful scarves and a

few wool stoles.

But she really needed to find the hat she was browsing for.

Upon gazing around, one captured her eye;

a golden hat with diamond stones.

She was flattered to see how nice it looked.

Fancy and rare, exquisitely cute.

Although the price was quite high, she was trying to

make up her mind.

"Finally, she took it home and, after a while, put it back on."

Suddenly, the hat began to talk and would not stop!

Scared, she threw the hat down to the floor and gave it a

shivering smile.

How can a hat talk? She was unaware of its magical bond.

Alarmed, she continued to listen to his words.

I am one of those magic things that happened to the lucky ones.

Do not worry, I am a talker and friendly hat.

Is it impossible for a hat to talk like a chatterbox?

You see, I was spellbound by witchcraft.

Who knows if the spell is still embedded in the stones.

"If there is any consolation, you are now the owner of a talking

magic hat!"

She thought to herself, what's wrong with having a magic hat as

a friend?

She changed her dress and wore her old-fashioned red shoes with

bows on the side.

Rubies and pearl necklaces adorned the night.

As she walks through the streets with elegance and strive.

Wearing her magic hat to complement her

most sophisticated attire.

The Seven Stones

When I was a little girl, my mother

used to read stories and

magical poems which would put me to sleep.

I never forgot a tale of ancient mystery

which I keep remarkably close deep inside of me.

Wondrous powers withheld by seven

stones, to be exact!

Never thought they would become

treasure tales and secrets from the past.

The dark green stone 'emerald'

with sparkles alongside, shaped like a diamond

clearly shining like a star.

It barely touched my hand, although it took me to the past.

I was trying to grow up incredibly fast.

The yellow stone 'citrine' with added silvery lines

marked the voyage, I was ready to embark.

A secret trip through the mountains away in a distant land.

The red stone 'ruby' showed messages of hope

all bottled up inside my fortune of future dreams untold.

The golden stone 'heliodor' felt warm to the touch

uncovered shadows cleverly hiding on top.

I was covered in jewels that rained on me like a parade.

But it was not enough for my happiness

because 'love' was a step away.

The blue stone "lapis lazuli" got tight in my hand

It felt like I was on an island all surrounded by sand.

I flew like a bird up and under the coconut trees

without a worry or fear flying forever free.

Floating on top of the clouds, the winds uplifted my spirit.

A glare of light shook my body

like a ball of fire without a sign or resistance.

The pink stone 'aurora' had to be touched heart-to-heart.

I was amazed at how I looked years younger than before.

The mirror was my witness. I felt an eternal glow

like the "Fountain of Youth," I was suddenly transformed.

The purple stone 'amethyst' was showing me the future.

I pictured my life changes through a tiny hole in the wall.

Many beautiful gardens wrapped around in picket fences

not yet lived adventures that stood out like a thumb.

I was accompanied by great family and friends

in my wishful home.

The black stone "obsidian onyx" empowered the

"Earth, Wind, and Sun."

Like the beat of a drum, where intrepid creatures ramble

free through vast forests.

The sounds of horses galloping as their beauty unfolds.

A pack of wolves displaying their survival skills

engaging in the hunt.

Butterflies never cease to appear, flopping their wings

in the pursuit of tranquility.

An amazing web of wired connections exists all around us.

It also brought sadness and injustice to a devastated world;

echoing down my heart like an angry volcano.

Inevitably, lava found a way to restore a new beginning.

Waiting for a sign of forgiveness, being worried and concerned.

I felt a strange feeling of tiredness,

like a river with "dried-up strength."

The world is ending! No peace, freedom, or love!

To keep us going through the balance of life,

a social, physical, and spiritual one.

Hope has inadvertently been broken; the passage left open.

"Evil takes advantage and steals our very soul."

The seven stones showed the beginning and the end!

"How can we make a change?" "How can we stop! The end!"

Unicorn

Oh! Majestic Unicorn, let your beauty show!

Graceful as a deer, crystal white as snow.

Hiding in the bushes, timid as a fawn

treasured by so many, hunted for so long.

Tales of legend still linger of timeless stories told.

About elves, leprechauns, even scary gnomes.

Happy little Fairies curious they approach.

Humming lullabies dressed in purple cloaks.

Lots of golden dust dazzling everywhere!

"In the heart of Rainbow-Land, where magic fills the air."

In every child's dream, Unicorns appeared

the rays of green and yellow fade over the years.

Misty smell of seasons in early winter morning

awake, the dragonflies dancing in the forest.

Caves of precious stones seem to disappear.

They belong to Unicorns, which travel every year.

Opened wells of river rock mark the way nearby;

when touched by their magic! That lives inside our fears.

Many stories dwell in our imagination.

Revealing emotions of long-lasting recollection.

Fairy tales amazed the world as raindrops began to fall.

Deep inside the rainforest where Unicorns are born.

Willow-Baba-Lee

On a stormy night back in the Town of Black Roses. It was the only place where black and blue roses bloomed. A tiny gnome by the name of Willow was born. He was to be the ruler of all the land.

Willow was growing and becoming extremely helpful tending to the growing fields and gardens. That is what they do; helping plants grow and being attentive to their needs. Becoming a subterranean goblin or earth spirit. Gnomes guard mines of precious treasures hidden in the earth.

He always wore his red hat and was already growing his long and hairy beard. His intuitiveness grew of everything around the land. Protector of all the plants growing in the surrounding plains.

One day as he was planting seeds in one of the fields, he found a huge ammolite stone. Sparked like the sun and shined colorfully in all directions. He put the stone in his pocket and headed back home.

He really did not know much about treasures yet, since he was still young. Although, he wanted to show it to his parents for their advice.

When he arrived, his parents could not believe the size and beauty of the stone. As they held the stone in their hands, it began to sing and dance. At this point, they knew the stone had special powers which they had never seen before.

Suddenly, Willow began to transform, touched by the spell of the stone. Growing at "remarkable height," he must have reached twelve feet tall. The parents got extremely worried and shocked as they straightaway hid the stone elsewhere.

Willow returned to himself as he looked at his parents in disbelief. They kept the ammolite stone hidden and hushed the incident from the other gnomes. Obviously, it could turn out extremely dangerous if it fell into the wrong hands.

Many years passed, and Willow had turned into an adult gnome. He was about to be crown ruler of the land. Willow asked his parents if he could wear the ammolite stone at the ceremony.

Willow was going to be crowned with the "yellow hat," which meant authority and power. More so, he was the sole heir of his family, and he would be entrusted to rule the Town of Black Roses.

The parents were a bit hesitant but being such a special day. His mother placed the stone on a silver chain and gave it to Willow to wear.

Everything was going well at the ceremony, and happiness was noticeable. However, in the blink of an eye, Willow began growing in front of the other gnomes. They became extremely frightened by his size, and they all promptly hid from him.

Finally, the other gnomes were peeking from their windows, terrified. He assured everyone it was fine, and he was not going to harm anybody. The gnomes could not understand why Willow had grown so huge!

But he began explaining the powers of the ammolite stone, which he had found in the fields. Likewise, it would have made me grow tall as a monster, but at once, Willow took the ammolite stone off. Somehow this time, nothing happened; he did not change back to his original size.

Worried and concerned, he did not know what to do, asking himself. Why am I not changing? Why is this happening to me? The other gnomes were extremely scared and shut their windows and doors.

His parents begin shouting at Willow, trying to grasp his attention. Therefore, they began screaming his name differently.

Willow-Baba-Lee, Willow-Baba-Lee, Willow-Baba-Lee.

Three times is a charm, and finally, the spell broke, and Willow returned to himself. He took a breath of comfort and embraced both his parents, that helped him break the spell!

Despite the unnerving situation, the other gnomes came out and cheer with gladness. From there on, everyone began calling him Willow-Baba-Lee knowing it wouldn't be wise to wear the stone ever again.

His parents took Willow-Baba-Lee back to where he found the ammolite stone. They guided him to bury it in the same spot where he found it to rid himself of the spell!

Afterwards, they wanted to make sure their son would not wear the stone ever again, hoping everything would return downright like it was. A peaceful and charming gnome little world filled with amazing   gardens.

Furthermore, they would never forget the beauty, enchantments, and mystery enthralled in the ammolite stone. However, after what they went through, surely, they never wished to look back.

Fiction

Angels in the Underworld

For centuries angels have made their presence known.

With messages or actual personification.

It is common to call upon an angel when in trouble.

Helpers of humanity for centuries and protectors of our lives.

They happened to be very aware of our difficulties in many ways.

"Angels know everything about who we are."

When a baby is born, we call upon their guardian angel

praying he keeps the baby safe from harm.

We walk through life targeted by events and

unexpected happenings we can't control.

Although, during disasters, their wings protect us.

Helping those who need it most by their willingness to shield us

from chaos.

"The underworld is a place of purgatory, an empty solace site."

A dwelling of empty souls who did not pass the test.

Many believe we are part of the underworld!

But that is all speculation.

"Fire descends like a windstorm upon the underworld."

"Where suffering and grief dwells through the spirit assuredly."

Angels exist there, too; they keep the order from those

who were not chosen to continue to the next level.

The possibility we are awaiting in a state of life cycles.

The continuation of lifespan in other worlds.
Even though, it is a confusing matter we always obtain,
the possibility of finding our actuality
or a metamorphic transformation.
Once going forward, defining the quality of one's consciousness.
Meanwhile, we need all the help we can find, to follow the way
and angels are the solution to the ultimate journey we need to
undertake.
Somehow, starting the long trip toward the
"Gateway of Heaven."

Beware!

By the magic cast iron sings.
Spells of lizards in the wind.
Fairies wear enchanting rings.
Diamonds fall out from their wings.
Wicked sounds beneath the stones.
"Awakes the monster in us all."
Beware! Not to whisper in your sleep.
A bewitching spell befalls indeed!

Crystal Ball

Looking through someone's soul
has been a family tradition
passed on from posterity.
Gifts provided by ancestors
from mother to child for centuries.
"Colliding head-on with destiny."
Scrutinized by those who do not understand the gift.
Sometimes, doubtful or misunderstood; however,
useful when trying to search for the truth.
Turn the lights off to let the candles glow.
Perfume to cleanse the air.
Flowers for the purification of the soul.
We call upon the spirits to communicate
beyond the physical world of material gain.
Apparitions start appearing
in the darkness of the night;
and moving forward toward the light.
Weird sounds of lost beings from an unforeseen divine.
Hard to believe our loved ones are standing in line.
Who knows if a haunting or a scary poltergeist?
The ghostly night begins to materialize.

As ghosts start marching in randomly.

They appear as they are called by their name one-by-one.

The importance of learning any good news.

Will I be rich? Will I be famous? How long will I live?

Can I see my relatives?

It intrigued us to learn the outcome of things.

A touch, a flow of wind behind our back,

spells and enchantments ready to be cast.

"Looking through the crystal ball creates a tunnel effect."

Traveling through time within our past, present, and future.

Paranormal activity continues during the spiritual mass.

The risk we always take is finding out!

What is behind the curtain? Knowledge, goodness, or evil.

Death

Thy riches, thy silver, thy gold,
will not stop! 'Uriel' angel of death
from dissecting your soul.
He really does not choose sides;
only goes after the balance of life.
When death is imminent, nothing can change its toll.
Believe in the irreversible intent of the spirit lingering alone.
Unstoppable desires and rudeness of the body and flesh.
But do not underestimate the brain.
For thee, I pray often; life has favored you in many ways.
Now, the ruthless truth inside us is painfully absorbed.
It can be the only way to pay for its decay.
Behold, bad intentions that bring us
face-to-face with death!
To some, we are just a speck of dust,
an insignificant cell in this huge bubble we share with:
humans, plants, animals, and everything in between.
As you climb to the top of the unknown, your body is just a shell.
Somehow, protecting the shrine of its worthiness.
What is more beautiful than death?
"Think of the unexpected and irreversible conclusion."

Nightmare

Staring at the ceiling of this empty, lonely room.

Looking at the colors of the walls.

Sorting out weird feelings of my emptiness inside.

I saw my wings open, and I began to fly.

As my spirit drifted away, it traveled to the other side.

Scared out of my 'wits,' I saw things that made me hide.

Remembering lost feelings somewhere, left behind.

Trembling down and restless of this dance that never dies.

Escaping from insanity in a world that does not sleep.

Waking up to noisy streets sounds like they never want to quit!

Steering echoes keep hunting me

as my mind storms through the past.

Wanting to put the puzzle together

but I only want to stop!

I keep running from myself like a scaredy-cat.

Finally, I woke up and screamed! What a dream I had.

"A secret state of mind."

The Power of the Phoenix

The gentle air brings a cool soft feeling to my afternoon walk.

As the wings of a Phoenix pass over me.

With his rich golden color that captures my attention.

Vibrant red feathers covering his enormous body;

which shelters his mighty force and beauty.

I have heard they have wondrous powers.

Especially their tears carry healing properties.

These creatures are a universal symbol

of strength, wealth, and riches.

Honestly, it is a powerful mythical bird

who has captured the interest of humanity for centuries.

The tale goes like this:

When a Phoenix becomes old and dreadful.

He will construct a nest of cinnamon and magical herbs.

He waits to hold on to the perch

until he turns into a ball of fire.

In a few days, a baby Phoenix will be reborn from the ashes.

He will grow to be a strong bird again.

I believe it would have been a privilege

to have met these remarkable and magical creatures.

Likewise, it is a legend which holds conceivable truth.

I can just imagine flying on the "wings of a Phoenix."

It would have been a wondrous experience.

(The Phoenix's magical powers even helped Harry Potter).

What a Scare I Had

How many of us dream but cannot remember a thing?

It happens to me all the time.

That is why I would like to share it with you.

Could it be a dream? Or a 'spooky' experience I had?

Last night I heard some noises

which shook me out of my socks!

My body trembling with fear

and nerve hiccups that would not stop!

I checked all over the hallway though I heard sounds

coming from the shack. With a flashlight in my hands

I wanted to check what it was; thereupon, frozen like a popsicle

my feet were fused to the ground.

My bones horribly shaking, felt my hands cold as ice.

My heart pumping like crazy;

it felt like I was having a heart attack.

Kept listening to weird noises as a light flickered off and on.

A window popping downstairs, clueless at what was going on?

I noticed the upstairs was clear, so I came down like a flash!

Something hit me on the side, but I could not tell what it was.

I went ahead to the kitchen even though everything looked fine.

The back closet was lit with only brooms and mops on site.

Suddenly, I heard loud screams!

From the back room echoing non-stop.

Besides, my ears followed the sounds through the

dark empty house.

The floor had traces of red stains, which stopped me

in my tracks.

Felt my knees buckled together and my eyes ready to pop!

When I reached the guest room, my jaw instantly dropped!

As I opened the door, someone shouted!

"Happy Birthday," my sweetheart.

Come and join the party, it is a special surprise!

"Well, I'll be darned," it is my birthday after all.

HA! HA! HA! What a horrible scare I had!

Furry Friends & Wild Critters

A Visit to the Jungle

Traveling through the African jungle
was an intimidating experience;
of strong essence and pure richness.
Impressive treasures and amazing power
which we need to acknowledge!
A wave of strength not to be reckoned with.
Extensive landscaping of soft lining and wildflowers
in all colors and shapes.
In the distance, you can smell danger.
"As beauty unfolds to the touch of the wind."
The air brings fragrance and excitement, just like a dream.
Animals lurking everywhere, looking for prey.
It is impressive to watch but scary at the same time.
Along the Savannah plains, animals can be captured
behind the lens of the camera
displaying their everyday instinct for survival.
In this beautiful country which I have had the privilege to visit.
Admiring every living thing that flies, crawls, or roams
through this lushes' land
which is really a breathtaking miracle.
This gorgeous place needs to be secured and safeguarded
at all costs.

The giraffe with outstanding elegance and long extremities

also, humble demeanor grazing at the enormous trees.

The impressive cheetah with its remarkable speed.

Lots of animals competing for a place in their groups

fighting and tearing limb-by-limb for respect from the pack.

Feeling the hot jungle breeze is a rewarding sensation.

Knowing how lucky I am to share

such an important experience with the animal kingdom.

Admiring the beauty and deep red soil

which holds an "old wives' tale,"

a sign of blood spilled of strength and power.

The presence of the lion was unimaginably impressive.

His roar could be heard from miles away.

The timid gazelle looked fragile,

despite always watching her surroundings and

ready to escape at any sign of an attack.

At the far end of the jungle, the herd of elephants

stomping away at the jungle's floor.

Lifting a huge cloud of dust

traveling together and eating away

at the hanging tree branches.

Such an impressive force from these

magnificent giants deserve our full respect.

As we continued traveling, the monkeys made all sorts of sounds

and the females nurse and carry their babies safely.

Nearby, the rhinos were preparing themselves for an attack.

Driving toward the lake, the huge crocodiles and hippos are

swimming very quietly.

"Only the top of their heads can be seen, and their big eyes are

rolling side-by-side."

After, the dark settles, and everything becomes silent.

The sunset disperses vibrant red, orange tones

as blue shades appear afar.

Not a light can be seen in the pitch-black sky,

only the eyes of the animals which become candles in the night.

My experience in the jungle was amazing.

A fantastic and rewarding exposure

which woke up my spirit and soul.

Loving the animals so much made me feel right at home.

Butterfly

Beautiful butterfly, how high can you fly?
Bursts of brilliant colors sparks of shiny lights.
As you flutter toward the sun your wings carry a pretty song.
Flying gently to the pond looking for flowers all day long.
Your display of pastel orange tones the morning as we awake.
Dust of dark blue and bright yellow turns purple into grapes.
Your precious crystal body lingers casually in the air.
I feel your distress when roaming a little scared.
I am always after your colors dancing in the wind.
Ageless is your legacy.
"Legendary is your theme."
For centuries you have traveled, and your presence will be
admired by many.
Asleep in a cocoon state until your creation is ready.
There you are, enchanting one.
What a privilege for my eyes to see!
Outstanding, is your beauty how lovely! Can it be?

Clever Cephalopod

A Greek word that means "head foot."
With eight-limbs and smart enough to use tools.
Three hearts and eyes that rotate independently
looking forward and backward for prey and predators.
The ocean can be a daunting place for their survival.
The females take very well care of the nest
as it is their final legacy.
Airing it constantly, making sure the babies are well protected.
Once they are ready to leave, they swim and fend
for themselves.
Swimming in an epic journey full of dangerous encounters.
His specialty is blending in using his muscles, which contract
dispersing thousands of pigment spikes called tubercles.
"Becoming the masters of camouflage."
He can pretend to be a snail, seaweed, or even a rock.
It changes color cells for his disguise, and if that fails
his ability to create a smoke screen as a decoy to
make his final escape.
Being the most sophisticated animal, finding an opened snail and
using it as an armor for his protection,
but now he has worked an appetite and
just in time for a delicious shrimp!

Cephalopods have a mind of their own; superpowers which help them survive in the treacherous and unpredictable sea.

Flower of Joy

Strolling through the forest on an early afternoon.

I stumbled on a rock that looked just like a bloom.

To my amaze, I realized then,

It was a baby turtle crawling away.

It dawned on me it was a boy

therefore, I had already named him "Flower of Joy."

I took him home and fixed him right up!

In a fish tank with pebbles, lights, and plastic plants.

Shedding a tear since he looked sad

would not even eat a tiny snack.

Pacing around like an anxious cat.

I felt quite sad and ashamed of that.

In the end, I took him back.

I placed him in the shallow water.

Afterward, he swam fast, feeling free at last!

In the wildlife home sweet home where he belongs.

(Please respect the wild.)

Forever Furry Friends

Waking up in the morning, my furry friends start the day.

Ready for lots of hugging and wagging their cute fluffy tails.

Jumping and going around in circles, catching toys in the air.

Such warm, smart doggies keep me going and content.

Sharing happiness together, I feel like a millionaire!

Never sad or depressed moments, they put a grin on my face.

As the day ends, a new beginning,

too much energy they express.

Whining at times for affection is just a normal way to say thanks!

I take them for walks in the daytime,

responding to my every command.

Barking away for acceptance, eager to say 'hello' to every

human friend.

Their endless love amazes me every day,

kissing and panting away.

It is hilarious how they behave with the intelligence they display.

My doggies are my faithful friends:

Tobby, Niño, Nana, Baby, Kyler, Kuki, and Luna.

Garu the cat and Sunny the Sun Conure, my all-time

feather friend.

True companions that will remain in the profound feelings

of my heart.

Handsome Tote

Well, even if I'm a bit ugly and some folks fear me.

I do not want to harm anyone.

Just string my tong for a treat to eat.

"No matter what people say, beauty is only skin deep."

To others, I could be hideous, but for sure, not to me.

I am too heavy to jump around, so I crawl a bit.

"Opening holes with my nose, I can hide when I need."

I love to be sprinkled with water when I am ready to feed.

"I can really be a handsome tote. You just have to

wait and peep."

With my clumsy, wet brown body, nothing ever frightens me.

So, when you see me in a garden or plainly in a tree.

"Do not stray away from looking."

You might finally like what you see.

Homestead Farmhouse

Long ago, I lived on a farm covered with fruit trees,
flowers, critters, and beautiful landscaping.
It was an early October morning
when I had opened my eyes to farm life.
Captivating smells of chickens, pigs, goats and
other uninvited guests were very unpleasant.
Living in the city for so long
was quite an overwhelming change.
On the other hand, I could see in the distance
nature at its best!
Twenty-five acres of sunflower fields
growing alongside, the aroma was a total blessing.
I would wake up to a peaceful kind of tune.
"Silent and serene."
Sounds of birds singing all day long,
a variety of wildlife animals visited the farm,
looking for tiny pellets left behind by the farm livestock.
The hens lay eggs all around the farmhouse;
so, the roosters impressed their cock-a-doodle-doo
throughout the day.
We all went about our business. There was always
something to do and no time to waste.

The geese were very selective; besides, not very friendly.

Rutty the gander always kept his group together.

He guarded the dames continuously;

except for Ruby, the 'chubby' one

doing her own pecking at whatever looked tasty.

As daylight approached, Ruby would hang out by the fruit trees

waiting for them to fall out. She loved to eat even out of your

hand.

As the day went on, I would clean their living quarters.

Their food and water bowls included, always making sure

everyone was fed.

It was a daily routine done before sunset.

All would fly and hide in the trees until morning

staying out of sight from night predators.

On the other hand, the lamb, sheep, and pigs

would lay in their stables waiting for the crack of morning light.

Living this kind of life was very pleasant,

a perfect stress-relief retreat.

Sharing my days with the animals, learning how to supply care,

and helping them grow.

It was the key to a balanced and prosperous farmhouse.

I would not hesitate to do it all over again.

Guessing, since I was born and raised on a farm

I just felt right at home.

(Love and respect animals. They are truly a gift from the above).

Hummingbirds

There is a spark of magic in the wings of a Hummingbird.
Precious and curious little bundles of joy
that visit my garden every day.
In the daytime, they look like birds
constantly flopping their wings.
But at night, they become tiny magical Fairies.
"Lighting the night in an enchanting dream."
As they fly through the forest, they hum soft sounds
which disappeared silently through the wind.
"Vibrating like musical waves in the distance."
They can even fly upside down!
Hovering constantly during flight.
Then, go into a torpid state sheltered
from the weather, standing on one foot on the perch as they rest.
They also chirp away to alert others for courtship.
Curious but shy, they appeared in precious assorted colors.
"They walk on my shoulders, waiting for a morning treat."
"Discreetly sip up the juices of berries, apples, and pears."
And, of course, I leave sugar water feeders
for them to quench their thirst.
These little creatures are a boost of energy.
I listen to their fragile songs whispering in my ear

"Hello, good day, I am here."

They appear and disappear like wandering ghosts.

"Now you see them, now you don't."

"Cute as a button but shy as can be.

I love to watch how they feed."

They spend time together by the blooming honeysuckles;

continuously, slurping away in hesitation.

Foremost, I love their uncertainty, which keeps them safe!

Bringing all kinds of happiness and love in their tiny wings.

Harmony can be felt everywhere when a Hummingbird invades

the garden.

"These flyers are an inspiring sign of hope and good luck."

Max

I have a cat, his name is Max,
and everywhere I go, he follows me.
He is white and black and wears a hat.
So, he can camouflage from others.
He loves to fish out of my bowl
as he plays with lizards all day long.
When he is ready to take a nap, he purrs and purrs
right on my lap.
I pet his head and sing a song.
He falls asleep and then starts to snore.
Unless he hears something outside
because his curiosity is improvised.
He will jump high and check around
then, he will call the "kitty-cat's meow, meow."
No matter what, I know he is a rambunctious kind of cat.
However, I love him no matter what!
My handsome feline, my little Max.

My Purr Friend Tiger

Once, I found a kitty-cat with personality!

His name was Tiger, and I could swear he often smiled at me.

He would tinkle in the toilet, even flush when he was done.

Jump in bed beside me and snuggled through the night.

A sloppy, slurped smooch touched my ear. "Tickle, tickle on my cheek."

He grabbed my feet. I felt his teeth.

A belly rub is what he needs.

"Meows and meows for my attention."

"Purring and purring for a tasty treat"

My heart regrets that he went over the rainbow.

However, his paw-print is still in me.

Nino the Adventurous

Walking through the market, I saw a tiny pup.

He was brown and white with a freckle on his paw.

"Playing with a ball bigger than his nose."

He would hide in a box begging for a bone.

He went around and bit his tail.

"Playful little pup indeed, I swear."

His name was Nino, "the adventurous one."

Always ready to have some fun!

He howls loudly throughout the day, asking to be hugged.

But no one pays attention to him, and sadly, he begins to shrug.

I know he's fed and has no trouble finding a bed.

However, he needs a safe place to stay.

"I remember how cute he sat waiting for anyone to play and pet his head."

When I called him by his name, he was sure to bark and jump with happiness.

"I really hope he finds a home and quits being all alone."

So, he would grow and be loved like he deserves.

Preacher Bird

One early day, I heard rhythms in the wind.

Then, followed all my dreams like a Preacher bird,

which gave me wings.

This little golden bird with silvery slippers and red velvet lace.

"Tweeted sounds of love songs perched upon a tree."

Singing away at a happy pitch melody.

I heard his message well. I am a "bird dreamer" at heart.

As he flew peacefully through the sky,

spreading joy wherever he landed.

His sermon felt sweet and long; my heart seemed overjoyed.

Special sounds of peace and love lingered in the winds of hope.

Sounds of a Preacher bird. I miss your company

because you understand my needs.

Always bringing sounds of music and

love into my life.

"Losing my husband was a bittersweet realization;

which tore my heart deep into the roots of its foundation."

Pumpkins & Lizards

Oh, veggies, you peek at me every morning
with the rising of the sun.
Pumpkin vines stretch throughout the hills.
"As in every flower, your beauty unfolds."
All your magic sparkles with a deep orange glow.
The lizards lay on top of your peel to catch some sun.
They even nibble from your stems filled with ladybugs.
Pursuing some ants for a tiny munch, between the leaves,
a grasshopper sat.
"Oh, evergreen vine you propagate in unstoppable style."
You grow to be remarkably huge.
"Therefore, we get to cut your eyes and mouth pattern for
jack-o-lantern's night!"
When Halloween comes, you become the main attraction.
"In every household, a table is adorned with good old-fashioned
pumpkin pie."
But the lizards hang around to keep feeding from your stems.
Which little crawlers find their way to become meals
for all those who wait.

Rutty My Goose

How elegantly you lay! Suspended by uncertain fate.
The ample size of your domain has changed
the smell of winter rain.
What brilliant colors do you display?
Echoing sounds of moving chains.
Oh! Ridiculous goose, my feathery friend. Stop!
Chasing dreams of yesterday.
Today is not a simple day.
Tomorrow won't be quite the same.
Hath found you out among the shade resting your poise
against the Willow.
The "womb of nature" feeds your nest.
The sun has risen on the meadow.
Only my love pours for my proud goose,
a great provider without question.
Enjoy what "Mother Nature" brings lots of good things
in her wings.
You will guard the nest and keep it safe!
Since your love for the flock is still the same.
"Every year, the cycle begins."
Baby goslings will hatch in the spring; as many as ten, I have
counted, no lie.
Congrats! My goose, my good-all friend.

Snowflake

One early morning after a cool November day.

I could hear my goat Lucy moaning, twitching with pain.

Right at five a.m., I saw his birth.

A handsome little goat white as snow

with a birthmark on his face;

Furthermore, it resembled a snowflake.

Trying to stand up was no joke,

stumbling to the floor many times more.

In the end, regaining his balance, but he looked wobbly,

just like a drunk.

As Snowflake regained his strength, I could see him standing

quite long.

Lucy attended to his needs like any good mom would.

He was looking for his mother's milk.

"Screaming! Loud, hungry, and confused."

Drooling out of his snout, the milk tasted so good.

Despite his ordeal, he fell asleep, closing his eyes were big and

round as he was resting during the night.

Lucy lay beside him, cleaning his coat and sharing her warmth.

The next morning when the rooster croaked.

He was ready to meet the other animals living on the farm.

Everything looked so pretty and nice.

He started playing around and listening to every sound.

Recognizing smells, you only find in a 'Farmhouse.'

He learned to walk behind me like a dog begging for food.

Jumping on the rocks, making noises with his hooves.

Already growing horns as he got me on the knee.

Stop! Silly little devil "Ow! You are hurting me!"

If you don't quit, I will not play or show you any more tricks.

I placed a bell around his neck so I could hear his every sound.

Eventually, Lucy kept a watchful eye,

always protecting him somehow!

She kept him away from danger, always closely by her side.

Someday, he would be ready to build

a family of his own seeking other pastures to roam.

Lucy loved his little Snowflake a whole bunch!

"What a precious addition to our farm home."

Sunny My Old Feather Friend

Long ago, right before my birthday, I received the funniest gift.

It was a baby Conure with shades of green, blue, and orange.

Besides yellow markings on his wings.

his eyes were big and round as he would look right through you.

But his tiny barely feathered body blended in to stay warm.

I named him Sunny because he looked just like the sun.

Barely two-month-old had to be fed daily by hand.

We used to laugh at the noises he made, chattering all day long.

He was quite loud in comparison to his tininess all around.

As time went on, he grew and grew and became colorful

like a clown.

He sparkled like the sun and glared like the moon

bounding down.

"I wanted him to talk, even say a word or two."

but no matter how I tried, he refused to learn a few.

I kept repeating words like baby, kiss, and even mom.

However, he was lazy and didn't learn a single one.

"Although, no vulgar words were allowed."

He grew so handsome and beautiful that he was the

talk of the town.

Other lady parrots would whistle and squawk at him sometimes.

Nonetheless, he would not look at them or even get aroused.

Even though, I miss him so very much, "we were partners; for twenty-five years to be exact."
Until one day, he fell asleep in an eternal bird dream and never woke up.

Twelve o'clock-Midnight Crow

In the silence of the night, listen to the midnight crowing.

"It lingers for a while to alert the hens to stay low."

Predators are in the area trying to climb the trees.

Looking for something tasty, watching out for the midnight treat.

He imposes his loud crow, alerting everyone to hide.

"The hens become prepared to seek shelter

as they stay out of sight."

The rooster protects its flock, whether in the daytime or at night.

But when the sunrise hits the morning, he continues

to guard his ladies and feed them grubs for his point-scoring!

For sure, they crow all day,

feeling their territory threatened at times.

He enters the coop elegantly and imposes his presence

when he climbs.

Protects every hen in the barnyard,

guarding everything on the ground.

He courtships them through the farmland.

As they get ready to lay their eggs up high.

Conserving the symbol of wakefulness.

He is believed to ward off evil spirits.

"Because of his vigilance and protectiveness."

Wolves

A pride of wolves is prowling about in the distance.

They are ready to exercise one of their best instincts, "the hunt."

Making no sudden moves, they all transfer to their positions.

Knowing who needs to be in front, rear, and sides.

It has been perfected through generations;

it works in a way that evokes admiration.

No time for errors,

only pure concentration as their abilities is enhanced.

Their strength is the most powerful tool the wolf needs.

But their intelligence is the important key element

which gives them the total advantage.

"Never underestimate the potential of a wolf pack."

Their spirit of hunting is the connection they have between

their brothers.

Everyone knows their place, and respect often

needs to be reinforced.

As they group as one is rare, their hunt attempt never fails.

Humans need to learn a lot from the wolf power, and

undeniable control.

Their impressive chain of command begins to shape with every

sudden turn.

*"Within The Alpha Male and Alpha Female," everyone else
needs to listen to the rules of the hierarchy.
Seriously, the way they live and communicate with each other.
It is nothing more than magnificent to watch.
"The pups are taught by example of the respect
toward supremacy."*

Wonderful World of the Seahorse

Soon after winter, I wanted to catch a drift around the sea.

I read a bit about the life of the Seahorse.

Amazingly incredible tiny horses that live on the ocean floors.

Surrounded by reefs of sea anemones creating colorful and

spectacular views.

I have seen them dressed in the most striking tones.

It makes the seahorse a perfect story to own.

They swim gracefully with such elegance which is shown.

Working hard to keep their homes intact in the caves they built

in the garden of coral and sea rocks.

You might not think they are fish; however, they are indeed!

The male carries the eggs transferred from the female and even

gives birth.

Becoming the main parent for the tiny babies in his pouch

as they grow.

More than a thousand babies are delivered,

but only five percent survive!

"Unfortunately, seahorses do not nurture their young, so they

must fend for themselves."

There are many species of these adorable creatures.

There are oddly shaped but interesting heads

that look like little horses.

"It seems difficult to believe they are remarkably fast."

Even their transparency glows like neon lights in the dark.

The spectacular life of the amazing sea.

General

A Star

Not everyone can become a Superstar.
But following the "North Star"
can for sure make you glow.
Not everyone is fit to fulfill their dreams.
But devoting a life to wondrous things
can help you achieve your goals.
Not everyone can climb to the top.
But being positive about yourself
can change the way you react.
Not everyone can be a celebrity.
But having a plan and seeing it through
can bring joy to those who seek hope.
Not everyone can find grace.
But knowing that somewhere out there.
Someone might see what you really are.
Not everyone can change destiny.
"But a little wish can sometimes be attained."
Not everyone seeks the right path.
But spending quality time with family and friends.
Can surely become the ultimate and extraordinary dream
come true.

A Quiet Place

When I entered the world of writing,

I find myself in a magical place.

Filled with every thought possible, I want to arrange.

My spirit wonders complacent up in the clouds, flying free.

"Exploring every idea and new paths of spectacular dreams."

I blow like a firecracker with each writing quote.

I search for a beginning and ending on a special note.

So, I can express in detail everything I wrote.

Some are memories or little episodes.

"Present happenings or events I can't ever let go."

Nonetheless, the essence of romance, fantasy, or even fiction

dwells in the depth of my soul.

Just like an evening bloom ready to show.

Inking every feeling that lingers in a quiet place

waiting to explode!

A Writer's Brain

I often realize that a writer's brain is filled with imagination.
"Unstoppable desires truly enhance the soft rhythm of thoughts."
Stories are built around the inspiration of the creative mind.
Time lingers patiently, putting phrases together.
Rhyming words of wisdom only a writer can write.
"A unique style of joining words and emphasizing
a particular moment."
Building beautiful chapters of poems, novels,
or even storytelling.
"Certainly, something you have lived through
or experienced among life itself."
A proud world of detailed poetic circumstances developed
between the years.
"Nothing stands in the way of creativity."
The present turns into future accomplishments.
The love for the arts is compensated for
"by the feelings of the writer."

Aim & Fire

Get ready to "Aim and Fire."

I have set my goals in life, and no one can ever stop me!

You have done your worst for me. Why can't you see?

Now is my time to win!

I am all together, battling any war

that stands in my way.

My dreams were swept away because I was in total darkness.

Now, I believe in myself, and I finally took my chances.

Get ready to "Aim and Fire."

The power of the angels is beside me.

To give me strength and guide me.

I will fight with all my strength.

I will become a warrior in the night

and my justice will suffice!

Despite my weakest moments.

"I will always find the light."

Beyond our Boundaries

Never have I been so certain of the power's we humans possess.

It lies dormant in the depth of our intellect.

The overwhelmed desire to uphold fragments of our imagination.

"Taken shape in the deep end of everything that surrounds us."

A perfect balance which helps us feel more stable.

Breaking the sound barrier with each sudden movement.

We are the most magnificent species molded by our creator.

Senses we still have not tapped throughout our evolution.

Firm believer of steadfast, unwavering resolutions.

Unyielding questions of future destinations.

The thought of total control of mind and body.

Psychic abilities within us trigger telekinesis.

Even mentalism or mental magic can be achieved.

Although, you might believe it is science fiction.

The efficacy of moving objects by the power of the mind.

"It is not hocus-pocus is a true phenomenon."

However, in some cases, it becomes a natural behavior.

*Furthermore, the mind must be taught, just like a sports player,
to become efficient.*

*Mysteriously and unknowingly, most of us hold the solution to
unlock the gifts.*

But the mind controls the power beyond our boundaries.

Christmas Eve

Christmas Day comes once a year.
Joyful moments of songs and cheer.
Presents hidden under the tree
awaiting the morning of great "Christmas Eve."
Candy apples dipped in glaze,
lots of goodies decorate our plates.
Mistletoe hangs from the chandelier,
for that reason, we celebrate this season every year.
Cookies and milk are placed down below
next to the chimney that echoes Ho! Ho! Ho!
Up on the rooftop, the reindeers await
jiggling loud in an old-fashioned way.
Everyone knows Christmas is near
preparing the feast for the family is clear.
Treats and sweets are set on the table.
It is the season of giving, and we do as we are able.
Children awake with anticipation!
To open their gifts on this one-year occasion.
Nothing can be more surprisingly neat
then to sing Christmas carols warmed up by the fire.
"In Heavenly peace."

Christmas is Here!

Oh! Shining bright star from the East, you have returned.
Our 'Savior' is born this Christmas Day!
In a simple Manger, he sleeps quietly
surrounded by cows, lambs, and little sheep.
Joseph, Mother Mary, and the Three Kings bow down
to honor the arrival of "Jesus, our Glorious King."
"Each one brings a gift to Baby Jesus:
gold, myrrh, and frankincense."
The goodness of Christmas is finally here!
Joyful moments will be enjoyed throughout the year.
Affectionate greetings and cheerfulness are clear.
Blessed be the miracle which we gather and cheer.
Family and friends travel from distant places
to share happy moments and truly warm embraces.
Hoping your Christmas brings special memories tonight!
And unforgettable wishes this year.

Emotion of Anger

Some of us see anger as hostility.

An annoying feeling, we sometimes do not know how to restraint.

Foremost, anger can be provoked instantly.

"No matter how much we tried to contain our anger, it is

stronger than us!"

Although, anger can be a good thing to release negativity.

It motivates us to find solutions to our problems.

When our muscles tense up, and the heart becomes rapid

for sure, we might be having an aggressive mishap attack.

Due to hormonal radicals released from the brain

it becomes difficult to overpower its domain.

Moreover, the wrath of rage is so strong we cannot prevent it.

Wanting to express ourselves and usually ends up in a fight.

For many years, I have tried to control my rage in many ways.

Even though, it's triggered by a turn of events.

By being cut off in traffic

or someone yelling obscenities,

our levels of anxiety shooting up to the roof; all these elements

can promote the overwhelming behavior.

A clever idea is to count to ten, breathe slowly,

talk about how you feel.

Helpful tools that can alleviate and help defeat these episodes and conquer anger!

Gardenia

"As my eyes captivate your beauty."
Yet, the smell of heavenly bliss lingers in the air.
White blooms of exquisite essence gardenia shares.
A touch of aroma overwhelms my surroundings;
leaving an exclusive smell of pure, sweet passion.
Wherever it rubs on, its perpetual scent is remembered!
The intense perfume of sweetness dwells as it withers away
by the touch of sunny days.

Garden Haven

As I walk through my garden, I am always amazed.

There lies a carpet of flowers that surrounds me every day.

As it turns into morning, they are replenished by the dewfall.

Sings of color in every petal as beauty unfolds like a whisper.

It feels like a sanctuary, a place where peace is born.

An enchanted retreat to let my spirit be restored.

In the middle of my garden, there is a narrow, muddy swamp.

It houses many birds and fish swimming along.

There is also a pair of swans secretly nesting in the hay.

They dance across the water gracefully, floating away.

In this magnificent canvas where seeds and blooms come alive.

The air is filled with exquisite fragrance

a site of content, a joyful relief, a breathtaking moment in time.

I see zinnia, cosmos, asters galore, plenty of pretty daisies

many wildflowers of all sorts.

Camellia, gardenia, jasmine and more,

sweet pea and sunflowers as orchids hung from above.

Beautiful butterflies flutter on top of the flowers

searching for nectar to satisfy their desires.

That is why I have called it 'Haven' because it is a very

spectacular place.

Where wonders happen each day.

"I thank God for blessing my hands."

For everything grows in harmony, plentiful, and grand!

Good and Bad Times

Sometimes, when things go wrong.

As life, somehow, may never change.

Somewhere along the way, the proper

choices were not made.

So, many times, the thoughts returned

seem never to erase.

There are possibilities and future dreams to compensate.

Somehow, I have heard so much

what "good and bad" is all about.

To aim high and take a step until we find our happiness.

The light will shine inside of us.

If you persist, it will turn out the way you planned.

Although life itself has a very unpredictable price.

Occasionally, when times get rough and

things do not turn thoroughly right.

To seek new roads, achieve new goals,

as to make a home a Paradise.

Nevertheless, life is just a covered box;

it is all a shocking surprise!

I have been there many times, I know.

That is why I can tell you why.

For the good times:

"Reaching out for something new."

"Brave enough to see it through."

For the tough times:

"It's never too late to start anew."

"Whatever wish may be obtained."

Because the good times are here to stay,

and the trouble times will go away!

Honky-Tonk Lady

As I was playing my guitar, I could not help but turn around.

There was a lady at the bar drinking away a Whiskey bottle.

It did appear she flinched her eyes

as I glanced at her once more.

She's just a honky-tonk lady, but for now she is in my song.

This good old country lady is the toughest girl I know.

Will strike a punch without remorse;

I know she's fearless to the bone.

Unafraid to start a fight, making you spin out of your mind.

You can't boss this babe around;

she will nail you to the ground.

Beware of her stunning punch, a nasty fighter holding a grudge.

Sometimes, she acts like a wildcat, totally looney, often nuts!

If she doesn't get her merry way,

she might shoot you on the spot!

She whistles at her black stallion to come to her aid.

Slamming everyone that stands in her way.

Then, she bribes the boys around town with blazing guns.

Riding away like hell as she hits the saloon.

Serve me a Whiskey bottle. I demand that you do.

Nothing can stop her! Not even the law.

This good old country girl, 'Betsy,' is her name.

"She's a gutsy Honky-Tonk kind of girl."

(The west was won by honky-tonk ladies).

I Know What I Want to Be

Once I was lost in the shadows, eventually, I found my way.

Couldn't be sure for a moment life could be so vain.

The fact that I look for a bright side, I pray every night

for good health.

God lights my way and shines upon me, for I'll never stray away.

Now, I want to improve myself; I just got to believe I can!

Optimistic when feeding my self-esteem,

never giving up on anything.

Walking through life's crossroads

with total sadness and despair.

Suddenly, change came along, blessing my life forever.

I found love in every corner in every step that I took.

I became brave and unstoppable!

With powers, I never knew.

Having strength in my soul, there is nothing to lose.

I will carry on tenaciously until I find what I must do.

The passageway is somewhat difficult.

Despite the fact, I refuse to give up!

Fighting for what you believe is not an easy job.

(A word of advice: do not be afraid to reach for the stars).

Italy

On my world travels, I wanted to visit Italy.
One of my nieces lives there, who I have not seen in ages.
It has always been my dream to take a
long and well-deserved vacation.
I had other places in mind, but Italy was on my priority list.
My goal was to visit Rome, Florence, Venice, and Napoli,
where she lives.
A time to admire the scenery of such a great country.
No rushing at all, wanting to enjoy my free time.
Strolling around the city parks, and their gardens
which looked amazing.
Of course, I am all about gardening!
Learning other cultures is particularly important to me.
Meanwhile, I want to explore their art treasures.
like the Colosseum in Rome.
The Vatican's most priceless art collections.
The Basilica of St. Peter and Michelangelo's artwork,
the 'Pieta.'
Duomo Santa Maria del Fiore in Florence.
Museo dell 'Opera del Duomo Cathedral Museum.
A gondola ride through the Grand Canal of Venice
the largest waterway.

Visit the Tower of Pisa Medieval stone carving.

When I arrived at Napoli, I wanted to visit the

Museo Cappella Sansevero,

The Ovo Castle and Royal Palace.

Also, order some of their Margherita pizza they are famous for.

After enjoying so much beauty but tired from all the

tour traveling.

I went back to the hotel to rest for the day.

I had mentioned I was an 'Author' to the

nice front desk employee.

Suddenly, after going down to the hotel lobby, I realized,

people were staring at me for no reason.

They were asking for my autograph, which felt amazing.

I had taken some of my book postcards,

which I signed up for them.

I felt a rewarding feeling being in a different country and getting

all this exposure.

But it didn't stop there.

More people kept pouring in to meet me and get my John

Hancock. It was surprisingly exciting.

Not only that, but I also had lots of fun!

And now I was getting lots of fans interested in my books, which

was nothing but unexpected.

I returned home although the family reunion, experiences, and site-seeing.

Will always be remembered as an unforgettable memory.

Legacy

With the passing of the years

I have experienced many unforgettable moments and

outstanding achievements, "my childhood dreams."

Many accomplishments met, others still pending yet,

but no matter what anyone says,

dreams can become a reality at any age.

I am totally satisfied with my endeavors; somehow,

is all about sacrifice and persistence, "reaching your goals."

Sharing love with my caring family.

Obtaining unconditional love from my four-legged friends.

"It's been an absolute blessing."

I have received many musical gifts

throughout my artistic vocation

and have benefitted in many unbelievable ways.

I really want to share them all with my supporters.

I have pursued music fields of study as a

musician, singer, songwriter,

and author of poetry by true inspiration and imagination

which I hold very dear to my heart.

"Believe when I say I have no regrets."

Life has been overly fair; exceptionally eloquent.

I swear I would not change a thing but give thanks

to the many challenges stored under my belt.

I have been showered with extreme possibilities

touched by 'Grace' itself, I am extremely grateful!

For all the wonderful years spent entertaining

audiences, meeting well-known artists and songwriters

from many parts of the world.

Great opportunities in life presentations,

shows, television appearances,

radio programming, and so much more.

Beautiful times shared with my followers in my lifetime.

"I will never forget my career attainment and performances."

(A firm and rewarding legacy is about life and living).

Men Cry Too

When a man cries, the feelings of weakness are perceivable.

It is a difficult reaction that dominates their mind.

They do not want to show fragility, only strength.

"Man, cry inside and feed their ego through a superior

masculine pride."

like an exaggerated machismo displayed in the tango.

No one knows why their attitude holds little sentiment.

But not revealing their despair,

a man's chain reaction is withdrawn.

Too many painful memories are kept out of sight

nonetheless, concealed in silence believing that.

"Big boys don't cry."

Masking their numbness hidden inside,

well protected and fortified.

However, sometimes their tears are heavy,

all choked up inside their heart.

"Oh, my! Why would I cry? I am a man, and man does not cry."

That is the way you were raised, and, therefore. Nothing can

change your ways.

"But it is perfectly fine to cry even if you are a man."

Tears are allowed here! Just let them fall.

Crying is not a weakness; it is a head-on collision

with joy and sadness, which needs to be reinforced.

Never-Ending Desires

Obscene desires hiding the truth in the shadow of the untold.

However, nothing can make me mourn.

Hope dwells in the threads of a lost and empty heart.

Hitting straight to the center of unkind and selfish roads.

Adversity against others always trying different gestures.

Moreover, pretending to avoid unpleasant revelations.

Silence is always a good weapon to brush off

malicious behaviors.

There is no one perfect or completely good.

To seek perfection is not as easy as you may know.

Sometimes, we need to look deep inside our soul

and ask ourselves.

Do we deserve the recompense of life?

Night Blooming Jasmine

It waits patiently with every passing hour.

A stream of little white flowers opened in the dark.

Carrying her exquisite smell called "the lady of the night."

The warm and tropical temperatures of the sun

gives her the perfect attribute to grow stronger.

Shrubs of dense and glossy green foliage turn to admiration.

When her flowers bloom, they disperse a night hello!

Her sweet fragrance has its presumption to attract snakes!

"More so, it's just a myth, a tale of untrue notion."

However, love is in the air when the flowers share its

passionate aroma;

which lingers in the night air for days.

She thrives like a beautiful queen in springtime.

I know it even treats signs of anxiety

by boiling some of her leaves and

even helps with the swelling in parts of the body.

"Always remember that plant benefits need to be taken

in moderation."

Night Jasmine symbolizes motherhood, love, and respect.

Purpose

For so many years, I have lived my life breathing,

eating, drinking, enjoying lovemaking,

arguing, aging, and contemplating the years go by.

Regular things we humans tend to do.

Sometimes, I ask myself, what is my life's purpose?

Why was I born? Why am I here? What does my future hold?

Questions which I have not found answers to?

Somehow, I will one day find the truth of my existence.

To make sense of it all.

No matter why I was born or why I am here.

It is to do good to others, help the helpless,

be a light in the dark, spread God's message and love

our neighbors. Likewise, these are the perfect reasons.

Who I am, what I am is irrelevant; furthermore, I hope

I can be a positive energy of imaginable strength and courage.

To be the best! That I can be is my true purpose.

Loving, caring, opening my heart to family and friends.

Who might have the same questions?

I am not sorry I was born! Of course not,

wanting to find out why?

It is just a human desire we need to accept, so,

I want to successfully become a better person.

Nevertheless, striving for whatever I was sent to fulfill is a

priority in my life.

Everything matters; charitable deeds, warm gestures,

unconditional love and being sensible to others.

Sharing knowledge and devotion; however, if I was

sent for a special purpose,

I sure pray I become the image of my Creator.

As when I pass away, I want to leave a final legacy

for my present and future stages of life.

Proud of who I am! Who I have become!

That would be, for sure... my "final purpose and my final

journey."

Quarantine from "COVID-19"

As frightening times embraced our lives

I pray for hope to get us by.

A chance to heal and be strong again.

For a new beginning, we trust to regain.

My guitarist friend called me the other day.

He and his wife got extremely ill with this flu strain.

I felt terribly sad sobbing for them!

Tears ran down my cheeks like October rain.

We had just gotten together to record

new songs, but it dawned on me

feeling an essence of concern in my bones.

Suddenly, I fell pulled to pieces, touched by this

nightmare that ripped our lives apart.

We were quarantined for weeks and beyond.

I saw my freedom slip away right out of my hands.

I asked myself how the world

would survive this horrific doomsday?

I really do not want my family and friends to die!

During all the confusion, I could not find any solution.

Unanswered questions remained unexplained.

Restrictions were imposed on wearing masks everywhere!

washing our hands and sanitized them repeatedly.

Staying six feet away even from our loved ones.

Worried and irrepressibly concerned.

I wanted to close my eyes and pray it would finally go away.

I did not want to believe what the "Bible stipulates."

I hope for no more new cases and hope for no more

senseless deaths.

A new rebirth free of disease for a healthy world once again.

(A little faith goes a long way).

Shout For Your Rights!

For life has spare unruly related matters.

My mind has wandered away and scattered.

Grass keeps growing indefinitely in someone else's yard

of troubled demeanor, which never seems to die.

"No evil power hath ever trod inside."

Your petrified urgency bequeathed my rights!

Strong hands have scorn "the impotence of man."

Shout loud, may your voice be heard.

Scream! To the world, may the roar enhance every sound with

steadfast concern.

No more! No less! Light for light.

"Truth for lies!"

Shouts of strong wind will forever be.

Superwoman

Woman of the past raging! Generations.

Voicing our opinion living limitations.

Achievers in a man's world ruled by wrong desires.

We need to change our ways and obtain what we deserve.

Woman of the 'present' demands and agitation.

Completing every task in different situations.

Working at all hours, meeting many deadlines.

Setting up agendas screaming for attention.

Woman of 'tomorrow' just like Superwoman.

Mothers of our children and mirrors of the future.

Trying to carry out good old-fashioned duties.

Bringing home support to make it all worth living.

Woman of 'conviction,' strong and open-minded.

Skilled in various areas inspired by every challenge.

Craving for success in this crazy world of madness!

"You are, for sure, a 'warrior,' and nothing can ever stop you."

Woman of the 'future;' call them Superwoman.

Always pleasing everybody, and family included.

Depending on ourselves striving for new careers.

Budgeting our lives and suppressing every fear.

"Woman of the 'World' we are truly Superwoman."

The Beauty of Music

Without the sounds of music.

Life becomes empty and sad.

"It feeds the mind and speaks where words fail."

A Universal language of peace; an enchanting rhythm scale.

Do Re Mi Fa Sol La Ti Do notes:

which improves our mood and range.

It makes us feel calm at times,

but fast tempo can arouse our brain.

Songs inspire our imagination.

Like an unbreakable chain.

"It is the best beat of my heart

that I give the Lord every day!"

The miracle of music can uplift our spirit.

"Believe in the power of love."

"Believe in the power of music."

The Fisherman

A fisherman's pride holds the 'key' to the sea.

The power of the waves nurtures his excitement to fish.

Although, between the sea and the fish.

The will to sustain oneself gives the fisherman.

"An opportunity of endurance."

Sometimes, he will fish for profit or pleasure.

But, to become a good fisherman, there are a series

of safety precautions that need to be followed.

"With every passive wave or unpredictable storm."

Undeniable respect for the sea needs to be shown.

Danger is what keeps the fisherman alive!

"The will to survive prevails."

The Lady in the Corner

Sometimes I feel like the "lady in the corner."
the forgotten one.
Sadden, by wrong choices made and now
paying the price.
I have no more tears to cry.
Only sorrow lingers in my heart.
Can anyone tell me why I am here?
Is this corner made for people like me?
Feeling lost, alone, and afraid.
Is this a punishment? Or just a leap of faith?
I guess is to learn what I am made of:
Strong will, unbreakable spirit, open-minded.
For now, I will keep living in the dark.
In the corner where I belong.
Waiting for the light to brighten my soul.
Drowning in a sea of "unprecedented events,"
looking for hope and change.
Soon, I will return from my dark past.
I pray I never have to go back.
A feeling of deep regret and remorse
awaiting to be forgiven at last!
Have you ever felt like the lady in the corner?

The Rose

I pricked my finger with the first rose of spring.

Sweet fragrance embellished my doubts.

Would I find love ever again?

Will it ever embrace my wants?

Will it ever follow its way to my heart?

"Sheltered by roses, I wait for the rewards of life."

For the wishes that can come true.

For the dreams still on hold.

For the time that cannot be turned back.

"Oh! My beautiful rose."

You are the memory that dwells in my soul.

You are the sweetness that stays permanently on my mind.

You are the consistent hope that will never go away.

The Sea & Me

For all the coral reefs, serpents, and seaweed.

For all the shells, mermaids, and fish.

Three million shipwrecks which lie down asleep

sunk and waiting for their destiny.

Sharks will tear you whole "in the wink of an eye."

Hungry whales feeding in the middle of the night.

In one breath is all I can recall.

"The Wonders of the Sea."

The place where strength grows boundlessly.

Sailing in the storm against all odds.

The will to survive makes me strong and powerful.

In the edge of darkness, the sound of howling roar

crashing against the sailboat with nowhere to go!

Foamy waves and salty air hit my skin

as the voice of the ocean speaks to me.

The strong waves made me feel free, but the sea cast a spell

in the "shell of my soulful."

The Sea

The sea holds many secret fables of ancient times.

Pirate ships, copper, and gold vanished before our very eyes.

Legend of mermaids, monsters, and electrifying eels.

Even strange creatures that cease to be seen.

Giant castles are built from coral, gems, and pearls.

Extraordinary caves of mollusk shells.

Many lives have been taken by the sea.

Bodies drift away, all wrapped in seaweed.

Inconceivable moments of desperation and fear.

It has touched those trying to find treasures

lost through the years.

Every day is a different tone of blue and the wind has

a soothing feeling of freshly new.

Groups of seahorse's dancing in symmetry.

Schools of herring splash in harmony.

Fish of all sizes and shapes swim at will.

Huge whales and dangerous sharks go after a meal.

Coins, artifacts, silver, and gold left from the past

still lie dormant, forever untouched.

The sea is an unpredictable chamber of beauty.

Mysterious magical seashells so pretty.

Wondering how it holds magic in the air.

With every color imaginable that glares.

It can be as calm as an afternoon breeze.

Yet, it becomes rough and deadly drastically.

But if there was a dream to become reality.

It would certainly be to live under the sea.

Tree of Life

By the Tree of Life, I sat one day.

Holding onto ideas that haunt me every day.

Sorrow struck my heart like a storm in the night.

Felt a knife cutting my flesh deep inside.

Hardship tore my spirit, betrayed, frail, and afraid.

Demanding answers, searching for change!

Abandoned in the streets, angry and suppressed.

Feeling a knot in my throat; thus, no escape

from the cell of hate.

Therefore, I tried to reciprocate but only found shadows dwelling

within myself.

A malfunctioning merry-go-round stuck in the same old place.

By the Tree of Life, I sat once again.

Felt wrapped in a bubble, ready to burst.

Will not let hurt consume me! Will not let pain prevail!

Time heals anger, hoping will cure my heartache.

Triumph will conquer at the end.

Finally, unwind my life from these heavy chains.

By the Tree of Life, I sat and sat.

"Baffled from all the affliction but at the end of the day."

The only thing that is still inside of me is faith!

Tribute to our Red, White, and Blue

During the midst of time, your sway calmed my heart.

"I love my Country, and I love my Flag."

It has strengthened my beliefs and has empowered my life.

Your peaceful celestial light shining with fortitude.

Against all tides and oppression.

"For the bravery and glory in which you stand."

For our fathers who fought for liberty and justice for all.

As we continue fighting to hold you "forever free."

Nothing can ever take you away from the spirit of your people.

You will always fly with solemn regard.

"Being protected by wings of honor"

Hold in profound respect in your presence and

wavering your red, white, and blue against all enemies.

With pride, I salute you every day.

"Give us hope and peace."

Wildflowers

The wildflowers have withered away.

Their smell is no longer intense.

The stems have dried out from the rain.

But the leaves keep falling from the long brown stems.

Nonetheless, the everlasting feeling

still lingers in my heart like the very first day.

"When they bloomed and left their essence in my hands."

Inspirational

Angel

I have sung you many lullabies.

I have appeared as a butterfly.

I have laid beside you every night.

I have rocked you to sleep and covered you up.

I have watched you grow throughout the years.

I have felt your every laugh and tears.

I've been by your side through perilous times.

I have shared with you a lifetime of wonders.

I have taken away your pain and sorrow.

I have watched you closely from above.

I have sent you signs I am always here.

I have kept you in my loving heart.

I will wait for you with stretched-out arms.

In the "Gates of Heaven."

As we will never be apart.

Baby Jesus

Keep your spirits high and your eyes toward enlightenment.
Call upon baby Jesus, he will nestle you in his thoughts.
Evermore, shield you with his power,
protect you always day and night.
He will give you strength and courage
mend your wounds and keep your calm.
He will cradle you at twilight
resting peacefully in his arms.
His love big as an ocean
washing away your grieving heart.
So, be brave my loving child
you will soon be back on your feet.
Keep your smile and wipe out the tears.
"Baby Jesus" is by your side indefinitely.
"Wow! He will heal you in no time."

Believe

Believe in his word and wisdom

lift your eyes right up to him.

Pray, he will take away your fear

as you will ride on the shadow of his wings.

Believe me, he is the rock of our foundation.

"He is the ultimate supreme reality."

The Being of perfect power and wisdom.

He has a plan for us, and we must choose

which plan or theme to keep.

"For sure, he will never forsake thee."

He is a loyal friend, teacher,

a loving father, and the best!

Pondering thoughts of "Christ's misery."

We would have given our life instead.

We know he would not want us to carry a cross.

He died for us and cleaned our sins.

Our lives should not be as important.

"As the one," who sacrificed it all.

Believe he is the yoke of our salvation.

His laughter is our joy.

He will gather many burdens upon his shoulders.

Still, find peace and rest in our soul.

Believe there are treasures in Heaven

just waiting to be claimed for a fact.

What must we do to redeem the price?

Get rid of bitterness!

Be more compassionate to others, and find riches

of our very own at last.

Believe thereupon, our eyes have not seen you.

Entrust, you will always walk by our side.

You will clothe us in total forgiveness.

Never leave your children behind.

Always believe that prayer gives us a better picture.

"What we need," "what we do not need."

"Who we are," and "our total purpose."

Do not judge or be harshly judged

for many bad thoughts and inequities.

We would not want to fail God's plan.

His understanding builds faith in our hearts.

Believe swords will pierce from Heaven.

Falling asleep in the hope of resurrection and everlasting life.

As we walk toward our place of rest. We will become richly

blessed.

In deep or shallow waters.

God would not let us drown; its trivial to imagine

our 'Savior' would ever abandon us.

We are his beneficiaries without a doubt.

With a settled heart we will be vesting in his delights.

Giveth my Love to You

Against all odds if forever thou shalt not pass.

Blindness has a loft for truth.

Oh! God instead nor, love nor, hate now all is done.

What's most dear to you?

Limitless, by affections anew make past offenses in lieu.

"I giveth my heart to you."

Heaven

What are the Heavens, I question you?

Is it a wondrous place to be?

Where people walk and fall in love.

Are the Heavens just like the stars above?

I wish someone could answer me

I need to faithfully believe; thus, in my dismay a glimpse of hope.

Who would I turn to?

Who would really know?

I grew attached to earthly things without thinking

life is but a wisp.

Wanting to capture everything out there

but in the end, all is written sometimes, not fair.

Now, I think more realistic like giving to others

makes me satisfied.

That is what matters upstairs I could swear.

The love you give is all you are allowed to wear.

As I wait for my angel's call afraid not if the dawn shall fall.

Knowing inside my soul will escape traveling straight to

Heaven's place.

Since I am asleep, I will fly all through the sky

and venture freely throughout the night.

As my spirit will soar in search of light upon Almighty Paradise.

I have earned my 'wings' in many ways sharing my life with

family and friends.

As in my passing, I will remember those.

Who asked, what is the Kingdom of Heaven

After all?

I Think of You

For every drop of rain that falls.
For every candlelight that glows.
"I think of you."
For every rainbow, near or far.
For every star that brightly shines.
"I think of you."
For every wondrous thing you've done.
For every wish that comes along.
"I think of you."
For every tree and grass that grows.
For every leaf that starts to show.
"I think of you."
For every bird that flies and sings.
For every little bit of everything.
"I think of you."

Inspirational Quotes

*"If you find yourself lost for words, dig deep into
your heart and express your true feelings."*

*"Don't ever feel alone on the road of emptiness
God is always by our side."*

*"Getting inspired is the instrument
of fulfillment."*

*"Secrets are quiet thoughts
placed on hold in our silence."*

*"What is a kiss? But the taste
of a nourished relationship."*

*"Where there are treasures, your
heart will find peace."*

*"Forgive my wrongs my cold heart
is to blame."*

"The morning brings the dew

and with it a new beginning."

"Play in the rain, make mistakes,
take the wrong train, until you lose yourself in God."

"Life is about challenges when we hit bottom
changes become the ultimate victory."

"If I have a story to tell
I've got to ink it."

"Acquiring wisdom is like
floating on top of the clouds."

"Building new bridges gives us the opportunity
to cross over more demanding situations."

"My paw friend went over the rainbow
but left an imprint in my heart forever."

"Faith is the bond between the soul and spirit
as; hope is the feeling between the spirit and soul."

"A wish is a flying feather whistling in the wind

trying to reach the whisperer."

*"Life is such a beautiful thing don't waste time
thinking about, all the wrongs of the world."*

*"Nothing is more important than the kiss you
leave on your child's cheeks."*

*"Lies can destroy life but truth
can put it all back together."*

*"We all wear masks but the
quality makes the difference."*

*"For the day to be so, ever bright
the night needs to show her presence."*

*"Vindicated and justified at one point
of our lives we found peace."*

*"Only through understanding are we
able to live with ourselves and others."*

"Behind our selfishness, we've arranged

to see life through the passage of humility."

*"Mommy I still see you through my eyes, I still smell
your scent in my arms, I still remember every kiss goodnight."*

*"How can anyone live with daggers
piercing down their throat?"*

*"A hint of salt can change our taste buds at once and
a hint of hate can do the same."*

*"Every choice we make whether good or bad.
It is finally added to our bucket list."*

*"Magic brings winds of
extraordinary miracles."*

*"The heritage of one's family is all about
joy, love, and endearing moments."*

*"We suffer from many wounds in life
slowly healing becoming scars that never erase."*

"As the years turned into memories no matter

how near, or far nothing is left to chance."

"No longer with my furry and purr friends.
But their memory holds a special place in my heart."

"Life brings many unwanted things, but it also brings
love and happiness which conquers all."

Jesus Lullaby

Now I laid right down to sleep.

I pray He will never abandon me.

Morning lights wake my eyes.

His Holy presence by my side.

With the beauty of summer days.

Rain and sun are here to stay.

In every breath, a flower grows.

Because it is the true miracle of love.

In the winter, freezing air.

I long for his endless embrace.

I hear his laughter and

seek his grace.

Alleluia, Alleluia, Alleluia.

Jesus will always live inside of me.

Listen

Listen to the rain that falls on my windowsill.
Come on and listen.
Listen to a baby's cry for a rock-a-bye.
Come on and listen.
Listen to the children play as their laughter
flows in the wind.
Listen to an answered prayer that will bind
the heart in love and care.
Listen to the lands of war without any hope
because love is missing.
Listen to the people's cry having to deal with
hunger and misery.
Listen to the homeless needs of a warm
safe place to stay.
Listen to a simple prayer that can save us all!
From anguish and hopelessness.
"Opened your heart and listen."

My Everything

Have you ever prayed for a miracle?

Have you ever lost all hope?

Have you ever cried in silence?

Have you ever praised the Lord?

Have you ever been afraid?

Have you ever called his name?

Have you ever gotten an answer?

Have you ever walked his way?

Well, here I am, my father God.

I am here to serve you and win over your love.

Make me whole and be my friend.

Take my hand and help me stand.

I know I do not deserve you.

I will remain your servant and prove my love to you.

Have you ever survived a storm?

Have you ever stood alone?

Have you ever lost your way?

Have you ever felt his grace?

When my heart is shooting love.

I pray I receive your blessings from above.

Because you are the power and our salvation.

"I am nothing without you."

I will clean your wounds and dry your hands.

I cannot live without your blessings anymore!

"My father God," I believe without you

"I am just an empty bottle without a cap."

Our Savior

Once, I was lost in the darkness, but eventually, I found my way.

It took some time as in my travels. I searched for "hope and

change."

Now I look for a new beginning as I pray every night

for good health.

Hoping your light shines upon me healing myself on the way.

Without you, my loving "Savior,"

hearts are aching and confused.

My life is now so much different because I found

your amazing truth.

As in my darkest moments feeling lost and in great despair.

You came along and blessed me always, taught me how to

become strong again.

I found faith in every flower in every breath of my life.

Creating new dreams for tomorrow, praying you will be

by my side.

That is why you are our "Savior."

"The one that will never leave us no matter what!"

Solemn Prayer

When I lay down to sleep

I pray to the Lord my soul to keep.

Resting in his loving arms

which will protect me day and night.

Please grant me health and blessings too.

"I will share it all I swore I would."

Thanks for everything you have always done.

"Giving me courage, that only comes from you!"

I serve you now with opened heart

my hands together in "Solemn Prayer."

Love will guide me through the night.

"Keep me safe so I won't ever feel scared."

Soul Message

For every moment we spent together

and all the happiness you brought.

Your memory soars inside my heart

with every single simple thought.

Despite I lost you forever,

your care over the length and breath,

never went unnoticed.

The pain will never go away.

I keep you close within my soul

giving me peace and rest.

Your humble smile and contagious laughter

resides inside of me like thunder.

I could swear your tears from Heaven

keep falling over me.

"I know God had other plans and took you in his loving wings."

I hear your voice in every song we used to sing.

Although, your presence is so ever bright

it lights the way anywhere and everywhere I might be.

The Perfect Song

Listening to a new song on the radio.

Its catchy rhythm got stuck in my head.

As it lingered on my mind it became hard to forget.

Suddenly, I imagined a whole different tune.

Heaven was pointing my way to shiny lights.

The tables had turned and

in the eyes of the world.

I heard whispers of significant importance.

I could swear it was totally an unusual song.

I heard ancient prophecies and vibrant sounds

that could reach as high as the 'universe.'

I could see in the background the moon, sun, and stars

floating together as one.

Even the "Milky Way" was following a different beat.

The planets were traveling at the speed of music.

Prayers appeared written in gold and bright silvery letters.

Bringing messages of divine inspiration and peace to all.

Every drop of rain, every spoken word, wrapped in love.

I could hear heavenly voices of 'angels,'

'archangels,' and 'seraphim.'

Altogether, in a sublime choir of hope for humanity.

The "Star of David" was guiding me through the entire song.

Congratulating poets, songwriters, movie stars,

musicians, and artists in general admiring their passion,

soul, spirit, and demanding work.

For their creativity and contributions which will remain in our

minds for eternity.

The real song I heard meant prosperity for humanity.

Proclaiming a new era of peace and harmony.

(Songs always inspire the soul).

The Tears of My Parents

As I opened my eyes for the first time.
I was greeted by tears of joy and happiness,
rooted in the hearts of my loving parents.
My tiny fragile body was cuddled up by the sounds of
soothing words.
Suspended, in total calmness, and bundled up in blue velvet lace.
All were welcoming family and friends.
"Everyone was trying to touch my little feet and hands."
A breathtaking feeling of angelic tenderness.
"A stream of light showered the overcrowded room."
Mom and Dad rocked the cradle where my tiny body rested in
peaceful sway.
A profound celestial ceremony; followed by the
presence of the multitude.
They are watching over my every single breath.
The tears of my parents would not stop falling!
Thanking God for the gift they had just received.
"My proud parents were so divinely blessed."
They had already chosen my name! "Jesus Emmanuel."

Wishes and Roses

Going around the world searching for peace.

Chasing every star that hides beneath my feet.

With a simple smile in a friendly kind of way.

Looking for a place to rest,

"I will pray and give my thanks."

Going around the world in the right direction.

Walking up and down the road bursting with motivation.

Dreaming of tomorrow and future expectations.

Living a new life free of worries and deception.

Going around the world with sturdy determination.

Facing every challenge with genuine imagination.

Daring to survive in this cold and heartless world.

We need to change our ways for peace to reign again.

Going around the world blowing roses to the wind

loving, caring, and pursuing every dream!

Even if some miracles might be out of our reach.

"Close your eyes and see the world like it was meant to be."

Romance

Bestowed Vows

Under the arbor of roses, solemn vows are bestowed.

The sounds of broken branches miraculously unveil our love.

Engraved in our hearts,

eternally brushed by silent words abroad.

Dormant in time sealed together,

our emotions awoken untouched.

Will you hold my hand, my love?

Lead me to the bridge of virtue.

There, life will intertwine our sacred vows.

Behold, by unforgettable memories.

We shall sail on a new journey.

Creeping thistle blowing in the blade of grass.

Helplessly surrendering our true love.

Look at me and open your eyes.

"For here I will always be."

Would you do me the exceptional honor

and marry me!

Everlasting Love

Your soft and tender kisses.
The long-lasting warmth you give me.
Has made the world around us
a magical place to live in.
As when I cannot be with you
I pray you are thinking of me.
I hold your picture closely
and long for you to hold me.
I miss your kisses every morning
how you are caring and devoted.
"A special love like ours is a gift from the pie in the sky."
inseparable by the love that grows and glows
in our perfect Paradise.
Your love and mine are all worth giving.
That is why we promised long ago.
"Always and forever," everlasting love.

For So Long

For so long, I've been trying to let you know

that I need to let you go!

Even though, it is going to hurt me.

For so long, you have betrayed my solemn trust.

Deliberately broken all the rules

in ways that I cannot mend it.

For so long, you have played the game of love

in someone else's arms; sharing the passion you once gave me.

For so long, you kept trying to come home.

However, it is best that you don't

let us not pretend to be with one another.

For so long, I have been trying so hard to know.

Why have you hurt me for so long?

But instead, I loved you more.

Garden of Wishes

Together we blossom like a delicate rose
charming each other in the circle of love.
In the "Garden of Wishes" where we met long ago.
Win over by dreams we can never let go.
Whereas our lips refuse to forget
on that special day when we kissed in the rain.
The moon and stars shined upon us
celebrating the days of 'yore' once again.
Life only knows it is hard to fall in love.
But a vivid glimmer of light sparks us with hope.
We will leave our print on the sand
walking down by the sea, holding hands.
Our love will play like a violin.
Shine endlessly, like a diamond ring.
We will climb mountains and swim in the dangerous seas.
But above all fly as one inseparably.
You and I will luster and weather well
building our passion as high as the infinite.
You as a 'garden' and I as a 'wish.'
uphold, by your love and my kiss.
There is a beginning, and there is an end.
Indeed, our spirits will never forget.
Worshipping each moment together, we spent
in the "Garden of Wishes," where our love will never end!

How Can I Go On?

When did it start? When would it end?

There is no way to tell.

Was it the way I looked at you?

Was it the way you held my hand?

But I found out you have someone else in your life.

Although, this love affair has gone so far.

We need to end these unforgiving lies and say goodbye.

So now, how can I stop? From loving you?

How can I accept this infidelity?

Should I pretend it was not real?

How can I live without you here?

How could I stand another day?

Nor withstand my broken heart.

How can I deal with letting go?

When I am irrevocably torn apart.

How could I cease my heart from loving you?

How could I let you go?

So, many memories we have built together.

So, many dreams we've shared along.

Now they are lost, nowhere to be found.

I cannot pretend any longer.

However, my heart is stuck with you.

How can I learn to love again?

And forget what we have been through.

I just do not know how I can go on.

I really do not know.

But somehow, we need to let go!

If This Is Love

So many days, so many nights
thinking of you deep in my heart.
I have looked around but could not find
a genuinely caring love endlessly divine.
If this is love, let it be mine.
I want to share with you, my life.
I believe our feelings have grown strong.
That is all I wish for from you, my love.
If this is love, let it unfurl.
Every word spoken truthfully shared.
Tenderness will be the essence left in our heart
our bond so powerful it will grow time after time.
If this is love will surely know.
Together for always, that is what we yearn for.
As the feeling of passion invades our body and soul.
Longing for one another is all we desire
and loving each other is all we must have.
If this is love, let it be ours forever.

I'll Be Waiting

When at times I get lonely, I wish you had come home.

Wanting all your love for so long.

As I sit by my window, I try not to cry.

I hope you are missing me tonight.

You know I long for your gentle touch.

Daydreaming of how you kissed me through the night.

I wonder if soon you will stay by my side?

When I listened to the sound of the phone ringing

my heart melts away because you are calling me at last!

For so long, I have been waiting for you to come home.

I am a very lonely woman without your caring love.

So, please tell me, honey, you will soon come to me.

You know I am waiting; I am anxiously waiting.

For your love to come through.

I will Catch the Moon for You!

Come rest your hand in my beating heart.

I will catch the moon for you in the glimpse of the night.

Hold Heaven in the palm of my hand.

Shoot a thousand stars and light up the sky.

Burning flames bursting through the tip of my fingers,

showing me the way to your holding arms.

Precisely, the reality that grows inside me

awakens a mountain of faith.

At the end of the rope, I close my eyes and touch your face.

I kiss your lips with the last breath of my lungs.

"I will love you today until the end of time, my love."

I will Catch You if You Fall

Near a millennium of unprecedented events

have drifted discreetly in the background.

Long waiting for distant experiences of everlasting coincidences.

Maybe, trying to make sense of all we encounter

every single moment of our lives.

"I know for sure you will catch me if I fall,"

in this life or in the next.

Your love is the only thing that does not lie.

My every thought and wish are to bring joy to my lonely days.

Your presence in the end sparks my life.

Through fields of mistakes and mountains of uncertainty.

"Your arms will be there to catch me if I fall."

Let's Be Friends

Let's be friends before we think of being lovers.

Let's take it slow until we know love is the answer.

Don't rush it through, I am telling you it's better this way.

Let's just be friends once again.

Will make it glow as the feeling gets strong.

It won't take long for the flowers to grow.

Reach out for the sun and join as one.

How two doves fly in the infinite sky.

"Will take it slow, you and I."

Let's just be friends.

We will learn to cope with one another.

To share our lives in many ways that's all that matters.

Will take our time. I swear it's better this way.

Let's just be friends until we are ready to become good lovers.

(Friendship sometimes works better than marriage).

Love

Love is a short word

which holds a powerful meaning.

Love grows deep within the fibers of our hearts.

A sensitive desire which cannot escape its power.

A force stronger than life itself.

It feeds our minds relentlessly.

Devours our senses like wildfire, burning non-stop!

Love can be seen in the silhouette of shadows.

Hiding as a ghost in the midst of the night.

The confusing pace of our existence

tends to blind the way we act.

Love pretends to make it oblivious

as we become vulnerable and distraught.

It slithers like a viper laying low for a chance to attack.

Makes us weak to the core and powerless to fight back.

Once you are trapped in his wings.

It will show who the boss is; and that is a fact.

Confused and helpless inside

trying to fulfill dreams the heart demands.

Another victim of passion gorged by an overwhelming feeling

that grips the mind and soul.

"The root of this word has existed for as long as we know."

It fools our understanding and feeds away

through every thought.

But love can be tricky, it can turn bad at any time.

Beware of its true power, a pure devil in disguise!

At times, a pretender becomes an evildoer to get what it wants.

Forcing itself as a host uncovering every stone

wherever it lands.

In other words, "Love can become the death of you."

Love Note

Your love came in the wings of a butterfly.
But it grew slowly in the wings of my heart.
A meaningful moment embraced our existence.
My darling if I could put the past in every step of my future.
I will live today every second of our yesterday.
Then I believe our tomorrow will be unforgettable.

My Amazing Love

Would you hold me in your arms and never let me go?

Does it matter some days I feel I cannot keep holding on?

Such a struggle I never really know how to remain

forever strong.

Although, I dry my tears and cry a little more.

"Because you will always be my amazing love."

I remember how you embraced me tenderly.

Wholehearted feelings with never-ending memories.

In my life, you are that special song

fascinated to never let you go.

In my dreams unbroken little star

that will always shine from above.

Believe, "God has a plan for everyone."

It is sad to say goodbye to the ones we love.

Every moment together, we have shared.

"Precious times and spoken words I cannot forget."

However, life flew away from you like a wild bird.

Though I feel you in this place, in this moment in time,

in my every sudden hope.

"My one and only amazing love."

My Special Man

I want a man to make me dream about him.

A special man who will know everything about me.

To share the love that I deserve and care for me in every way.

To make me feel just like a 'queen'

and turn my Paradise into a dream.

I long to find that special man I don't quite know how, or when!

Someone told me long ago that wishes often would come along.

I pray I'll find my dream man today, tomorrow,

but soon someday.

"For to find a thoughtful man is like finding a

needle in the hay."

I want a man to make me sing

and make my world new every day.

To make me feel sexy and take away my miserable pain.

I want a man to make me shine but if I am down to lift me up.

A special man, a gentleman, my special kind of man.

I want a man to make me laugh and hide surprises in my heart.

I want a man to serenade me when I am

worried or feeling down.

I want a man to give me flowers little gifts before I stress.

I want a man to warm me up to hold me close tight in his arms.

"As in my prayers I'll thank the stars," for granting me,

I want a man to embrace my wants and never let me go.

Where would I find that special man? Where could I find him?

Please tell me where because frankly, I don't have a single clue.

It really can't be that hard! To finally meet my fate for once.

But if at last, I find him, I swear I will never give him up.

He will dwell inside my heart in perpetual bliss.

My Valentine

If I could not find words to say I love you.

They would be written in my mind forever.

If there were no tears left to cry

But sadness in my heart.

I would like to share with you my every moment.

Even if the sun refuses to shine

or romance runs out of rhyme.

You will always be inside of me

in every thought of my life.

Because you are truly my one and only Valentine.

I have been waiting for your love to arrive.

You have opened my eyes gently and bestowed

your love upon my lonely heart.

I have dreamed about this a thousand times!

"I solemnly swear my love to you until the end of time."

You are today and eternally.

My true Valentine.

Remember Me

Open your heart, let my love in

as it cuts through my veins deep into my skin.

Open your heart and let our love be heard!

As high as the mountains springing down to the sea.

Open your heart; I pray that you do.

There is not a day that goes by I don't think about you.

I clearly remember the first day we met

walking down "Heaven's Highway."

Love was ever-present in the air.

Dreams and memories which kept us alive

now, dwell in the sorrow when you died in my arms.

I felt your absence in my heavy heart.

Life ran away from you during the night.

I always remember how happy we felt.

Perfectly made for each other like fools from another world.

It was like magic falling from the sky.

We had surrendered our love in the glimpse of an eye.

Blessed by the power of two loving hearts.

How strong our love endured when our lips met

for the first time.

They were sealed by a kiss of passion

presently lying dormant in the past.

Until we meet again someday, for sure true love never ends!

"Remember me, my love."

Song and My Guitar

It is incredible how a box with some strings

can create such beautiful melodies.

Regardless, songwriting has always been my forte.

But being able to play the guitar

has, without any doubt, completed my artistic package.

Thinking about it seriously, a musician has a key role.

Creating notes with different instruments

until they flow together in a unique harmony.

"A masterpiece evolves."

My guitar was an incredibly special birthday present

from my better half.

When I play her, I think of him, in fact,

I wrote a song in his memory, "I Want to Love You Forever."

I am grateful for his gesture which has

opened many great opportunities.

"Thank you, my love."

My guitar is a piece of jewelry

I care for her by changing the strings,

tuning, and polishing her so she can shine!

I need her as much as she needs me.

I named her 'Mamasita.'

(Nickname my husband picked out for me.)

Surrender

To the many challenges we have lived through.

To the many questions we never found answers to.

To the many wrong turns taken impulsively.

To the many opportunities we shared with each other.

To the many words we found to say, "I love you."

To the many beautiful moments, we spent together.

To the many notes we sent to one another.

To the many mistakes that taught us good from wrong.

To the many prayers which saved our relationship.

To the many smiles we gave every day.

To the heartbreak of losing, you until I surrendered to my loss.

To the many times we had to say, "I am sorry."

To each second of our lives in perfect harmony.

Over the many years, we learned about faith and hope.

Surrendering our pride for the sake of love!

Thinking About You

All my wishes came true when I finally found you.

I was hopelessly lost before I felt your love.

Now, I am thinking about you.

When I dream, I am with you in your arms very closely.

Though you are trying to hide your emotions

inside and I often do wonder.

However, we cannot ever forget what happened between us.

I know you are afraid to commit, but when you go away

I feel your indifference.

You will agree that no matter what happens.

I will always be there.

Oh! My darling, I do not know how can love make us

hurt this way?

Once it grows deep inside our hearts, there is no escape.

Even if love is restrained by infatuation or make-believe.

Between the demands and the musts, it will not let us go.

Because this is love even if you are lost or in disbelief.

You know I will always be there, and my heart swears

"I'm still thinking about you."

The Heart Does Not Forget

Our hearts will not forget the years we spent together.

"You for me and I for you," in one single breath, join forever.

Our hearts will not forget how we made each day

a little brighter.

Between sweet words and loving thoughts

our burdens became lighter.

Our hearts will not forget trailing down difficult roads.

Never giving up on "wishes or hope."

With buoyant attitude, we made bold choices

as we surrender our hearts to love one another.

I will never forget how we giggled for just anything.

Enrolled in a carpet of snow, we sat in front of the fire

drinking wine in a peaceful winter throne.

What! Unforgettable moments!

"The heart does not forget so much love."

Our hearts will not forget every emotion we felt.

Throughout the test of time and in the still of the night,

we stayed the same.

Limitless, our love grew steadily like a blossoming rose;

caressing each other in a cuddling embrace.

Our hearts will not forget the wonderful life we have shared.

We are tested, we are challenged, we are encouraged.

As we unraveled every chapter of our lives

surrounded by the true "miracle of love."

We became blessed in the heartbeat of time.

"How can the heart forget so much love?"

Without You

Without you, my heart has dried up in sadness.

Without you, nothing is the same

even the sound of the ocean has become motionless.

Without you, my days turn into nights and years silently pass by.

Without you, I can still smell your fragrance lingering in my

empty room.

Without you, my mind dwells away trying to catch a glimpse of

our memories.

Without you, I am sometimes lost in a world of uncertainties.

Without you, I feel my heart dying softly with every heartbeat.

Without you, I miss every moment we shared together.

Without you, sometimes I cry myself to sleep,

and my tears vanish in silence.

Without you, life turned dormant,

but my will is pleasantly strong and compelling.

Storytelling

Alfred's Island Curse of the Leopard Witch

Called it mysterious or a hoax but after many years Urban Legends are still the talk of travelers. Visitors that love to experience haunted places. The tale of the Leopard Witch began long ago on Alfred's Island.

A lady herbalist by the name of Catherine Cook. She was the keeper of the town's pharmacy and began preparing herbal and holistic brews. Besides natural remedies, she would create special teas out of plants and roots. Her mother taught her the science behind these powerful natural medicines.

One day the Town Mayer got extremely ill, and after trying many old-fashion antibiotics recommended by the town Physician. Catherine believed an herbal substance she had created might help cure the Mayer, and she gave him a cup mixed with lemon tea.

"Unfortunately, that same night, he passed away in his home." The town was infuriated by the news. They considered Ms. Catherine had given the Mayer a dose of poison.

She was taken to prison and without any trial the following morning they hung Ms. Catherine in the middle of the street in front of the Mayer's office.

It was a horrible death sentence imposed on someone who wanted to save the Mayer. Different opinions varied amongst the town citizens. However, that terrible decision would come to haunt them forever.

For many years weird and spooky incidents kept happening around the town, near the woods. Inexplicable sudden death, especially to those who belong to civil services or appointed to the Mayer's Office.

Many town folks kept to themselves. Avoiding talking about the Urban Legend. No one really paid much attention to the gossip around the apparitions. "Of a Witch dressed in leopard skin, sharp fangs, and dangerous claws."

Anyhow, many of the schoolmates laugh and carry-on whispering stories of unfounded evidence of the curse. Nevertheless, two students became fascinated to dig into the past. "Additionally, find something truthful about what really happened to Ms. Catherine."

The students packed their backpacks and headed over to Alfred's Island. Both rode on the ferry to be transported to their main destination. Ready to challenge their friends, yet excited to draft the best essay on such an important story.

Soon they arrived as they headed to the Downtown district. Staying at Alfred's Breakfast Inn. They wanted to be close to the area and begin their investigation regarding the Leopard's Witch Legend.

Finally, both began walking down the forest trails. Around midday, they rested for a bit and in addition were confronted by a mountain lion who was up on a hill, into "attack mode."

In the myth of the confusion and trying to evade the animal, a leopard woman appeared. She looked savagely violent and, with a ferocious disposition, attacked the mountain lion.

Scared, they sought shelter in a nearby deserted wood cabin running for their lives. Trying to hide from getting killed, they went inside the cabin and closed the door. Evermore, listening to the savage roaring outside.

After a while, everything quieted down as when they opened the door to their surprise! A woman who looked like a leopard was standing in front of their eyes.

Somehow, being confused, they couldn't find words to describe her. Nonetheless, the leopard woman told them these are my woods, and I do not welcome strangers.

The students could not tell if she was human or an apparition, she had pointed ears, brown polka dot pattern skin like a leopard, a long tail, sharp teeth, and a bad temper. This ghost was grotesque, displaying a nasty attitude in an attempt to explain why they were there?
She signaled the way out and said you need to leave at once because if you do not I will gladly turn both of you into shreds. Merely one mile away from the motel as they moved quickly away from her.

She then explained being plagued by evil spirits which turned her into the creature of the haunted woods. On that fateful day when I was hung till death, evil spirits took my soul, and transformed me into a leopard Witch to punish those who took the law into their hands and hanged me. As the evil spirits had their own cause to hate the Town Mayer from past injustices.

They strolled down the path and promptly arrived at the exit away from the woods. Her presence was felt every step of the way. Both girls left at once in shambles for all they had seen. The Witch message was obviously clear.

Without further hesitation, they ended up at the entrance of the trail. Hopping on the ferry, leaving everything behind, as they left Alfred's Island for good! Now they had sufficient evidence to write in detail what really happened to Ms. Catherine Cook.

"Although, the curse of the leopard Witch apparitions continues in Alfred's Island." The University students realized it was more substantiated by "Corrupted Power," and "Obstruction of Justice."

Pixie Land

Long ago, in a faraway land lived five Pixie Fairies. They were the nicest and cutest bunch you had ever known.

Each one had a special power starting with Amarina, the oldest. She could transform water into ice. Fabrina, the funniest, was able to change objects into whatever she wished. Londrina, the intellectual Fairy, was always using her magic to control wind, water, and fire. Biodrina, the smartest and most sociable of them, used her powers to see into the future. Finally, Kudrina, who was the pretentious of the Fairies, was able to change any unpleasant situation.

They all lived very happily, sharing their wonderful personalities, and making sure everyone was safe in their Mushroom Town called Pixie-Land.

All the homes were incredibly unique in shape and extremely colorful. But on the other side of their town, there was a thorn wall. It had been built ages ago and separated them from the danger of Troll Town.

Their neighbors were big creatures of unpleasant habits which always posed a threat to Pixie-Land. For many years they kept the Trolls at bay, turning back when they tried to leap over the thorn wall and getting stuck with painful needles.

More so as years went by, they would constantly try different tactics to claim ownership of Pixie-land. They were gruesome creatures that needed to stay away from the beautiful town.

Thankfully, the Pixies' powers helped and encouraged them to keep their distance. However, they constantly were creating new and sophisticated artifacts to overpower us. They will never have the chance to claim any rights to our beloved land.

Some days, the Pixie Fairies would scout the arean making sure everything was as it should be. One day as they were visiting a nearby Fairy, they noticed that something was wrong. Everything was out of place, and Fairy Nirvana was nowhere to be found.

The Pixie Fairies were very worried since she would never leave her home. She had everything she needed right there. They started checking around the forest to see if she was hanging around the pond. Besides, they could not find her at all.

They went back home and alerted the town about the situation. Once they heard the shocking news, they were all alarmed and proceeded to go look for her, joined by even the animals that lived amongst them.

After many hours searching, they ended up near the thorn wall. When the other Fairies flew high to check the other side in the distance they could see Nirvana inside a magical enchanted cage. The Trolls must have trapped her and taken her away.

Our poor friend Nirvana was locked up, scared and trembling. We were all upset, not knowing how she ended up as a prisoner of Troll Town?

Stung by this terrible discovery, everyone got together to find a way to free Nirvana from the Trolls. We had to get help from the powerful "Wizard by the name of Herod." He lived in the southernmost part of the forest.

But we knew for sure if we asked him, he would agree to help. Since he never liked the Trolls and for years, he had many unpleasant encounters.

So, we flew in search of him with the hope we could find Herod soon. Flying together through miles of intrinsic trees growing as high as the sky.

We finally arrived at his shack which was filled with weird hanging bats as well as spiders that gave us willies. We knocked at his door, and a big-hooded man answered. We asked if he was the well-known Wizard by the name of Herod?

He nodded with his head and said yes, who is asking? We introduced ourselves, explaining what had happened. He told us every other year. The Trolls imprisoned Fairies. They performed a Witches' ritual for their town to stay prosperous.

She did not have too much time left! Oh gosh! Would you be so kind to help us get her back? Herod explained it was a very risky adventure, but he was up for it.

He grabbed all his tools and embarked on the trip to Troll Town. After a day traveling non-stop, he finally reached the town. The Fairies were by his side in case he needed their help. Herod lifted his magic cane and lit up Troll Town like it was Christmas.

He storms through the street, pointing his cane at whatever stood in his way. The Trolls were frightened by his presence, and most of them hid in their caves.

Soon enough, others were trying to put up a fight and began growling at Herod forcefully. However, his power was too strong! As he continued defeating them one-by-one.

Meantime, the Fairies went to aid Nirvana and, with a flick of their wand, tried to open the cage but it was enchanted by the spell of the Witch. Unfortunately, their magic did not work! They moved the cage to the other side of the thorn wall and went to seek the forest Witch to help them open the cage.

The Witch would have to use her own magical powers. Flying over the forest they got near the Witches' cottage and asked her to please release Nirvana from the cage. The Witch wanted to know, why the Fairy was locked up in her cage?

We just learned the Trolls stole your cage to lock up our friend and use her in a magical spell. The forest Witch became enraged as the Trolls had stolen from her many times, but she had already made a Witch potion to set a barrier for the Trolls, keeping them away from her domain for good.

She then lifted her wand, saying a few Witches' riddles. She finally opened   the   cage.

The Fairies gratefully thank the forest Witch for freeing Nirvana. Finally, they flew back to Pixie-Land. Overjoyed with the relief that nothing terrible had happened to their Fairy friend.

Herod was still fighting the good fight and speaking magical words to destroy the Trolls. The remaining ones fled away as Herod vanquished the Trolls with his mighty magical cane. Destroying them one after another.

Thanks to the power of Herod the great Wizard! Everything returned to normal, and the Pixie Fairies were in debt. Thanking Herod for all he had done and especially for saving Nirvana. He told them that whenever they needed him, he would always be ready to help!

The Fairies then flew away to their home. The whole town was waiting for them with joy and happiness. They continued living a harmonious life but always paid close attention to the unpredictable Trolls.

Soroa the Killer Fungus

One afternoon a group of friends got together, planning a hiking trip to the mountains.

They had been talking about it for months, however, they were all busy with finals. Consequently, could not find the time to go. Therefore, they needed two more weeks to finish all their exams.

They discussed the possibility of making the trip, which was three hours away in Georgetown.

James, Marie, Johnny, Lydia, and Hector were packing their bags overjoyed with excitement. In fact, Hector did not really want to go because his girlfriend was ill. The group wanted him to join them but after Hector called Savanna, his girlfriend. As she insisted that he should go.

They packed heavily, making sure to have everything they needed including an emergency first-aid kit. Since hiking is a dangerous sport and at times the terrain becomes hazardous. It was a clever idea to be cautiously prepared.

They also grabbed perishables, rope, and lots of flashlights. They headed down the road singing in the car, thinking about the exciting and relaxing time they were going to share.

They had rented a cabin near the mountains with plenty of rooms for everyone. After many hours of driving, they stopped at a gas station to refuel, everyone bought some snacks including lots of beer.

The man at the gas station recommended that they be careful climbing since it had rained a lot for the past month. The grounds were very drenched and slippery.

After getting their snacks and fueling the car, they continued their trip toward their destination. Singing along anyway, talking about the adventures they were going to experience. Finally, they arrived at the cabin, it was deep in the woods but a beautiful site.

James and Marie wandered around the place; it was breathtaking. Moreover, they could see a creek peeking off the side of the cabin. Johnny and Lydia went down a slope and toward a fire pit, an awesome spot for the s'mores tonight!

Hector was following them and stepped off a rock that had a weird substance attached to it which he had never seen. It looked like crystallized insects were stuck to it. However, he tossed it out and continued walking toward the slope.

They could not wait to walk through the wood trails and reach the mountain area. Hiking was a long-lived passion for many years and all the equipment was ready for their journey.

Not a moment to waste after they settled in, they filled their backpacks with plenty of supplies. Knowing it would have to last them for two days immediately began walking into the woods. They rested a bit; it was sundown, so they began building their tents and all sat to watch the fire.

Getting ready to call it a night, all was very calm and peaceful. Only the crackling sound coming from the wood fire could be heard. Hector was ready to retire; he was the first to say goodnight. But suddenly, he could see a weird slithering white substance coming toward him as it grabbed his foot and dragged him inside the woods. He was screaming and trying to get it off.

Although, the white slimy substance would not release him, he ended up next to a huge tree which was covered in the same white slimy substance as it crystallized him in a matter of seconds and covered his entire body completely.

It was eating his flesh; he was not able to free himself and disintegrated. James and Marie followed his screams, but when they got close. The screams faded away, no one could find their friend Hector anywhere!

Johnny and Lydia ran to them with flashlights and scoured the area but could not find Hector at all. It was like he had vanished from the face of the earth.

After a while, they were exhausted, certainly needed a break. They asked each other if this was all a prank? You know Hector is a prankster. Therefore, they went back to the camp and waited for him. Despite the fact, they did not hear or see him.

Obviously, they were getting quite worried. So, they began searching for him again in the woods. Going down the creek but found no sign of him.

Johnny mentioned it would be ideal to go back to the car. I bet he is laughing at us right now, while he hides away. Somehow, as they tried to exit the woods, they found themselves back in the camp area again, like they were going around in circles. It just did not make any sense.

Searching in his backpack, Johnny found a compass but was going haywire and they had no signals from their cellphones and felt trapped! It was getting dark and there was no sign of Hector.

They started a fire; to warm some of their canned goods, no one had eaten anything all day. Marie mentioned it would be better if someone stayed up and watched over the camp. They needed to make sure the camp area was protected, the group agreed, and Johnny took the first watch.

Something was moving closer to Johnny. Concerned, he stood up and checked around. But it looked like a rabbit was moving in the bushes; he just needed to keep his friends safe!

It was close to midnight, and a full moon; he could hear the wolves howling constantly. Nevertheless, he was feeling quite nervous, but the noises from the crickets were especially bothersome.

Suddenly, a weird sound was approaching, and Johnny was figuring out what it was. It sounded like a slithering noise coming from the woods. For a moment he thought it was a snake. Otherwise, he went to investigate, and could see the bushes moving and swaying back and forth.

A white slimy substance went after him; he tried running away from it. However, it was upon him and covered his foot, crawling on top of his leg; he could not free himself from this white web smothering and burning his flesh with no escape! It was too powerful, overpowering him totally wrapping his body like a mommy.

Johnny did not even have the strength to scream! It crystalized him like it did Hector and finally disintegrated him to nothing.

Right at daybreak, Marie woke up looking for Johnny but couldn't find him in the area. It was weird since he was watching over the camp. Marie wondered if he had gone down to the creek; she woke up Lydia and James. They began calling his name but there was no answer or sight of him anywhere! He had also vanished just like Hector.

Lydia told the others it is time to walk out of here, and alert the police of what is happening in these woods! They picked up everything and put their backpacks behind their backs.

They started walking toward the path where their car was parked. Lydia was crying heavily, missing her boyfriend Johnny so much. I do not understand what is happening here but if we stay I am afraid the same thing is going to happen to us. They walked for miles and took the wrong turn. Somehow their compass did not want to work.

Likewise, they saw a flag wavering rapidly in the wind. They realized a military cabin stood on top of the hill. It was all fenced in like trying to keep something out! There was a bell hanging from the post, so they began ringing it.

Someone peeked out of a window, telling them this was private property. None is allowed inside, can't you read the signs? All began screaming at the same time, telling the guard we were in trouble.

Please, we need your help! We have already lost two of our friends.

Oh, help us, let us in, we just need to contact the authorities to help us find our friends. We tried calling with our cell phones but could not find a signal.

The guard went downstairs and opened the gate for them. He also supplied some water to drink and the phone to call the police. Marie called the police station, explaining to the officer what they had experienced. We need to find our friends right away!

The police told the group to stand-by where they were until they got there. Afterwards, the police arrived as they described all that had happened. They wanted to go back to the same area to check it out.

Marie told them they had lost their friends Hector and Johnny; in the campground where they had slept. One of the police officers began checking the woods while the other went down the creek but no sign of either of them. They called for reinforcements and began searching through the different trails.

However, the officers could not find the boys at all. Nor any clue of their whereabouts. Marie and Lydia were overly concerned about what was going on. We cannot understand where they could be.

The officers assured them; we are doing everything possible to find them, so please, do not worry. We are doing our job. They needed the underlying cause of their friends' sudden disappearances.

James told Marie and Lydia to stay, he was also going to join in the search. One of the officers found a pair of eyeglasses by a huge tree. but when he went to pick them up the white slimy substance poured out of the tree as it grabbed his hand rigidly. He was fighting to release himself, screaming hysterically.

Fortunately, he had a knife in his pocket and sliced a piece of the white blubber, cutting it so it would come off. Everyone ran to the officer thereupon, finding him almost unconscious; his hand all wrapped with the white slimy substance which was giving him a lot of pain. He felt cold as ice.

The ambulance was called to pick him up and take him to the hospital. They could not get much information from him. His condition was critical. The other officers continued looking everywhere for Hector and Johnny.

Despite all the unanswered questions. The officers realized that something very unpredictable was lurking in the woods. A very mysterious thing responsible for the attacks.

They needed to find out right away what was hurting people. It took the officers many hours to realize the teenagers weren't coming back; regardless of their efforts.

So far, they just did not know what was triggering the events. Two officers went to the hospital to check on their partner. They needed to find what attacked him.

The Chief of Police Goodman asked for help in this urgent matter and gathered a few more officers and sent them to the woods with a special unit, which dealt with these types of cases. He also ordered a Canine Unit to help with finding Hector and Johnny.

So far, no one really knew why they had vanished without a trace. However, they were collecting more evidence to complete their investigation. Everyone pulled together to find the teenagers. Trying to solve this unpredictable unknown disturbance.

Marie, Lydia, and James did not want to leave the camp believing their friends could return. Terribly upset and worried, thinking they would never see them again. They still had not been able to call none of the family members and give them the terrible news.

The officers kept perusing some of their leads and got a call from Police Chief Goodman to stay in the camp area and try to figure out what was going on. Six officers remained on the scene to help with the search and rescue making sure no one else would disappear. Since, at nightfall is when the teenagers had been snatched.

It was close to midnight, and everyone was tired. The officers told the group to stay in their tents and get some sleep. Two policemen began lighting the fire pit and stayed up on watch.

Eventually, all was calm, the noises from roots and trees began to sound. It felt very eerie and frightening, the unnerving situation was taking a toll.

The same white slimy substance was coming closer and closer. One of the officers lit a tree branch to burn it. However, the Fungus began to react and squealed out of control. Somehow, they knew at that point it did not like fire. Suddenly, it moved away from us and into the woods.

We were lucky it did not attack us, but we knew for sure it was not going to stop! The assault on Hector and Johnny was the unmistakable evidence. The officers called their office and spoke with the Chief of Police Goodman.

Then explained they were dealing with an unknown organism which was living in the wooded area, hurting people. What could be done to solve this problem, they asked? A scientist team which would have the knowledge of how to restrain it.

He called and asked for help in this urgent matter. Immediately a science team responded to the scene. A Doctor by the name of Edward Sore and his helper Dr. William Atkinson became aware of what had happened to Hector and Johnny.

Even one of their officers was still in the hospital. Now they needed to find out how to get a sample of the unknown substance. Learning exactly what kind of organism they were dealing with. For sure, it was an aggressive one. Two people were missing, and a third in critical condition. Edward Sore and William Atkinson had some of the substance attached to a branch.

Dr. Sore bagged it and took it to the lab. They were careful not to get any of it in their skin, they needed to investigate its properties. They took a small sample and placed it under the microscope.

They could see many different cells rapidly shifting from side-to-side very aggressively. Likewise, trying to overpower each other, they had never seen this before. Its properties were not from the earth; they suspected it was not a normal Fungus.

They kept on checking it very carefully and named it the Soroa Fungus since they had been working in their laboratory with another type of Fungus called Horizon also picked up from the same wooded area.

Consequently, it was not an aggressive kind. Soroa showed signs of enormous complexity and aggressiveness. They had laid the branch in the counter and still had traces of the Fungus attached to it.

Suddenly, it began to crawl from the branch and managed to go after a rat inside a cage. Instantly, the rat became covered with the Soroa Fungus; her entire body was crystallized.

They burned the remaining Fungus with a torch to prevent it from killing the other animals; nothing made much sense. Where did this substance come from? Why was it killing?

They were sure it had spread through the woods. How to control it? The scientist had many questions, but the most important one was. How to stop it!

They contacted a very well-known scientist that had dealt with unknown Fungus in the past and would most probably know what to do and how to exterminate it. His name was Henry Nottingham working at the Dells Laboratory and Speaker of much innovative research; a Professor from the Stanford University.

His knowledge was needed to learn how to remove this rare and dangerous Fungus. We called him but he was away in his Country Estate in New Hampshire. We left him a message that was vitally important to call us as soon as possible.

The next morning, when the phone rang, we spoke to Dr. Nottingham, explaining all about the Soroa Fungus and how dangerous it was. Dr. Nottingham recommended that we not get near it until he was able to examine it. As he arrived Dr. Nottingham began examining the Soroa Fungus.

He told Edward and William he had never met such an aggressive Fungus. For sure it needed to be quarantine from everyone it was not a normal Fungus its properties were unheard of.

For the safety of humanity, it needed to be destroyed at once. It goes after flesh and blood to survive until he eats away the host as it becomes crystallized.

After they heard this horrifying news, they had to produce a plan to destroy Soroa. Even though, the question remained of how to trap the Fungus without leaving anything of it behind.

They all knew it was going to be a great challenge, but it had to be carried out right away before any more victims were affected. We had to call a specialized unit with the proper equipment. They had to be extremely protected with special suits that the Fungus could not penetrate.

However, as they were planning to exterminate Soroa. One of the police officers left to secure the area and advised that Soroa had grown triple in size and was heading toward the Downtown area, suggesting it had grown into a humongous ball of slimy blubber.

As everyone was running for their lives. It was dreadful to watch how it would crystallize the town citizens on the spot. Everyone is running from Soroa's uncontrollable hunger creating panic and chaos in the streets. They had called the Army to destroy the slimy mass ravaging everyone in his way.

The town citizens were screaming in agonizing terror. It was an overwhelming and intense situation.

The Army tried to corner it on a dead-end street but began climbing the wall to the other side and escape through a hole in one of the tunnels which connected to the water reservoir.

The Army personnel kept trying to find it but Soroa evaded capture and slipped away toward the woods again. They needed reinforcements, automatic fire torches to be able to destroy it. Although, press for time they did not want Soroa to hide again it would get more complicated to find and kill it.

Dr. Nottingham had an idea to lure it to the far end of the woods where a cave without exit had been used in the past to store train parts. If we could trap Soroa in the cave it would not have a way out and we could finally blast him for good.

The trick was how to get Soroa into the cave; it would not be an easy task. We must plan a bait to entice Soroa to follow it into the cave. Once we have it cornered it will be easy to finally exterminate it. Sore told them to just use him as bait no worries, I am strong and a good runner.

Soroa would come after me then burn him with the torches, it was the only way. He began walking around the wooded area where they suspected Soroa would attach itself.

It was a matter of time before Soroa aimed at Sore. He began slithering toward Sore as he was luring him into the cave. Soroa was a step away from him. But he managed to enter swiftly and Soroa ended up inside the cave.

The Army man blocked the entrance so it would not escape. Sore was trapped inside with Soroa as he tried to exit through the back of the cave but there was no opening. They began torching Soroa as it began blowing up in size again.

Soroa was completely engorged and shrinking drastically until it turned to dust. Sore and Atkinson needed to make sure Soroa had been destroyed totally.

After searching, no traces of the Fungus were found anywhere. They checked all the wooded areas making sure it was exterminated.

Sore said this nightmare is forever over! He spoke to the Chief of Police Goodman and told him everything had been taken care of.

The Soroa Fungus was finally obliterated. We also made sure to investigate all the areas and found no signs of it in the woods.

But a month later, Soroa the killer Fungus was found again. It was attached to the wings of a bird crystalized by the sea.

The African Spirit

Throughout my lifetime I've had all sorts of dreams. Some were very pleasant, but others scary and mean. Knowing it is difficult to remember all that we dream. But for some reason, the one I am going to share felt like a truthful reality.

One stormy night before I went to bed, I always read a chapter of the Bible. It usually soothes my soul and makes me sleepy. I could tell I was falling asleep right away.

After a few minutes, I felt myself sweating profusely becoming agitated without any cause. I began to cry while asleep, desperately fearing something was about to happen to me.

As I continued to snooze, I heard a bang at the door. I was too drowsy to open it, so I pretended it had been my imagination. However, seconds later, I heard a loud knock on the door once again.

I glanced around the bedroom besides, everything looked fine. Suddenly, the door opened by itself very slowly. I'm listening to the creaking noises it made. I began sweating again and shivering with fright.

I wanted to open my eyes, but they felt heavy and burdened. Instantly, I saw a ghostly figure close to my bed. A tall shadow with a huge headdress crown of feathers hanging like a waterfall.

He was wearing a wooden bow and arrow resting on his back. He had other weapons, but I could not tell very well in the dark. Therefore, I sat in the bed, and could see his face clearly.

On one side he was covered with holographic markings across his features. On the other side was a horrible skeletal scene. Bones gruesomely protruding from head to toe.

I felt my heart was about to drop! I realized this spirit wanted to communicate with me. Likewise, I could not understand what he was saying. "It appeared he was speaking a foreign language."

Despite being scared and confused, I just wanted it to go away. The minutes felt like years, my breathing had accelerated instantly as my hands felt frozen stiff.

Even the room's temperature had dropped drastically. I was blowing smoke out of my mouth same as in wintertime. It looked like a scene from a horror movie.

Since I could not understand him, he started using body language moving his hands up-and-down and side-to-side. He was pointing his wooden staff forward, and he wanted to be followed.

I was in complete shock from his gruesome appearance, but even if I wanted to walk between my shivering and trembling, it became impossible. He persisted that I should go after him.

Anyway, I was shaking all over thereupon, using his magic staff to lift me up. I found myself levitating throughout the house. He stopped! In the middle of the hallway, looking all over the house as if he had lived there before.

Perhaps, in another time, recognizing every inch of the property. He was paying close attention to the pictures of the family, hanging all over the walls.

I felt very tense and fatigued from the whole ordeal. But afterwards, I continued levitating.

As we crossed the last hallway finding myself at the back door which led to the backyard. He took me all the way to the far-end of the lot then pointed his staff on the ground where a huge Oak tree was planted.

In broken tonged he assured me he had a treasure buried in that same spot many years ago. He told me his name was Shaka-Zulu and his father's name was Tribal Chief Shikany.

He was showing me when he was a young man, and his father had given him all his riches in a big treasure chest. Malecki, his servant, was listening to their conversation. Whereas he managed to learn where the treasure was hidden. Later that night, he had stolen it! Selling some of the treasure to pirates which were sailing away. The rest of the jewels and gold coins he buried in front of an Oak tree.

The next morning when they went to search for the treasure, it was gone! Chief Shikany was outraged and began looking for Malecki. He sent his warriors to find him, and when they did, made the servant kneel in front of Chief Shikany. He imposed a severe punishment on the servant's life. He was to be buried alive! Scared as he was, pleaded for his life but found no mercy.

The Tribal Chief Shikany ordered the members of the Tribe to dig a hole for the servant. Before sunrise, they took him to the site and buried him alive. But before dying, he cursed the Tribe:

"With the same wrath, you are burying me
I curse your souls never to be free.

You will linger forever and find no peace.

Until the curse is lifted, I swear indeed."

Everyone was dying from an agonizing death. Therefore, the Tribal Chief called upon a Witch Doctor from a nearby neighboring Tribe to rebuke the curse.

Unfortunately, it was too late he received the news that his son Shaka-Zulu had died. Sadly, the Chief fell to the ground in subbing tears. The warrior explained that when his son was walking through a jungle path. A lion attacked him and ripped his throat right off. He became devastated and did not know what else to do.

Everyone kept dying in terrible ways; he realized that greed had killed his son. He fell into despair, missing his son so much, he did not have anything to live for; so, that same night he took his own life! The Tribal people began perishing gradually until there was no one left, and the Tribal land died off.

After he finished the whole tale, he confessed that the servant had been killed by his father in a horrible way. Although, he needed to find the treasure so it could be returned to the Tribal Land and finally, break the spell! Since his death, his spirit had never rested wondering through the past without being able to find his everlasting peace.

"Knowing everyone had died cursed by greed." We all did wrong by imposing such a detrimental death to the servant. Eventually, we all paid dearly for our actions. "Foremost, back in those days, the punishment for stealing was death." My father, Chief Shikany, was just following their strict Tribal laws.

He wanted me to dig up the treasure, it was the only way to put an end to the curse. Somehow it had to be dug up at night and could not be opened at all. Accordingly, if the chest were to be opened, the incantation would linger on. I knew how desperate he was, wanting so much repose.

Finally, I agreed and told him I was going to help him out. But under one condition only and "I made him promise me." Once I dug up the treasure chest, he was going to leave me alone and never return. Shaka-Zulu agreed and thanked me for helping him find peace.

When night approached, I began digging a huge hole in front of the Oak tree. Exactly where the spirit showed me, I dogged for hours without resting. The treasure chest was very deep, and time had pushed it even further down.

I touched the corner of the chest with the shovel and began breathing heavily. I knew that I was close, I could see my hands bloody and full of blisters from all the digging.

By any means, at this point, I wanted to end the curse so his spirit would finally be free. I kept digging a bit more until I uncovered the chest. I was incredibly careful keeping it as secure as possible. For some reason, the temptation was overwhelming. It was like an evil presence was forcing me to do the wrong thing.

Thinking it could have been the servant's spirit trying to stop me. I am battling with all my strength, but the entity was too strong. Inadvertently, there were intense winds a tornado was passing through. I was struggling to keep the chest close, just like instructed. Despite my effort, it opened by itself.

I didn't want to look inside, but the pressure I felt in my neck was excruciating. Someone wanted me to see what was hidden in the chest; therefore, the curse wouldn't be lifted. Fighting with the evil entity was difficult enough until I felt complete domination.

I was too weak to keep avoiding the unavoidable as my eyes saw what was inside the chest. I felt defeated thinking about my failure to Shaka-Zulu's spirit.

When I saw what was inside, I could not believe it! "The most grandiose treasure I had ever seen it was so bright it even hurt my eyes." Immediately flashy rays started flying out of the chest in all directions.

I was horrified because it looked like a powerful firestorm. Burst of rays of all colors and shapes. Overwhelmed by the outcome, I wanted to escape but my feet felt stuck. I wasn't going anywhere, whatever was making this happen was invisible.

I could only see rays and sparkle of lights pouring down and burning my hands. I was desperate to be released from the firestorm, which was out of control. Somewhere, out there, someone had other plans.

I fell to my knees and putting my hands together I prayed for salvation to please make it disappear. A stream of light surrounded my body and protected my soul. I felt peace in my heart once again, and when I closed my eyes, I was back in bed.

Although, when I checked the next morning. My footprints were still printed on the soil in front of the Oak tree. The house floors still had traces of debris from the backyard leaves.

The only thing I can think of; most definitely I had a true encounter with the spirit world. A complete out-of-body experience for sure! It's hard to believe spiritual things can happen even in these modern times.

But I am telling the story from my heart. "It is up to you to believe it!"

The Ghost and the Serpent

In one of the ancient, abandoned Towns of Bartolome. A wandering ghost from the past appeared often. People had seen him off-and-on in the cemetery. Certainly, a ghost that lingers in a constant place is in search of something left behind.

He kept appearing and disappearing in the same area of the City of Ruins. Sometimes residents from the close-by town would leave flowers and candles thinking the ghost needed some attention.

One day three little girls went by the solace place. They wanted to hide-and-seek in the abandoned graveyard, which was the perfect isolated place to have fun! Holding hands, they entered the City of Ruins, and not far away was the cemetery.

Lots of places to hide, so they began to play. One of the girls began counting while the others hid. Instantly, they heard weird noises coming from the tombstones. They were scared and started running away from the cemetery as fast as they could.

But one of the girls fell and hurt herself and could not walk or stand. The other girls did not even look back; they just kept running and screaming. The little girl was crying and shouting for help. She was still not able to move, and she moaned with pain.

In the distance, a huge serpent was slithering out from one of the tombstones. She was terrified and began shouting, but no one could hear her. Since the cemetery was extremely far from the town where she lived.

Desperate, she managed to crawl over the stones and into a patch of squash vines. But the serpent kept slithering toward her as she closed her eyes and hoped for the best! Abruptly, a ghost appeared and placed himself in front of the serpent.

The ghost looked straight at the eyes of the snake and forced it to turn back. When the little girl opened her eyes, she was able to see the ghost up close for the first time and was no longer scared but thanked him for saving her life. The ghost told the girl that the serpent was not going to harm her.It was simply curious since no one ever visited the graveyard. He was a harmless serpent and loyal friend foremost, looked a bit scary.

The ghost explained that when the City of Ruins became uninhabited. Lots of animals began to roam all through the grounds. It was the perfect spot for the wildlife to gather moreover, eat from the delicious fruit trees.

The ghost asked the little girl what her name was. My name is Jasmin, but everyone calls me Jade. So, she asked him for his name? The ghost replied; I am called Savic Nano. It is a little strange, I know. "But I was named after my father and grandfather."

The little girl asked why are you still here as a ghost? Well, it is a long story, but to make it short, I died when I was twelve. I fell from two stories high and broke my neck. Oh, my Lord, that must have been terribly painful.

To tell you the truth, I did not feel a thing just happened too fast. Although I passed away, I was not ready to die. That is why I keep lingering here until the time comes. The little girl could not understand. She was totally confused.

She asked; how much longer do you have to live here? When will you know when the time is right? I will not, but an angel will come to visit me and let me know. I have never talked to a ghost before.

Usually, it is very scary. Otherwise, I do not feel scared talking to you. After a while, the serpent appeared and brushed beside the little girl. She asks the ghost; does he have a name? Of course, everyone has a name! His name is Slit.

Whoa! What a short name, and it starts with the right letter; S for snakes! She giggled, and they continued to talk about themselves. Jade had to leave because her parents would be worried. The ghost told Jade you are always welcome here anytime. I get very lonely; I only have my friend Slit to talk to.

Do not worry, I will come back sometime to chat with you. Jade waved at the ghost and the serpent and went back home. When she got to the house the family was asking what had happened. Seeing her all bruised from the fall. Yes, I fell and twisted my ankle and could barely stand up.

But your friends came and told us you stayed behind. They were extremely fearful of the weird sounds coming from the graveyard. You know very well that we have told you not to wander around the City of Ruins because it is not safe! Jade told the parents that she was fine and there was nothing to worry about.

The little girl did not want to tell the parents about the ghost and the serpent. She knew they were not going to believe her, so she kept her secret deep inside. The next morning, she gathered around her friends and told them the whole story.

The girls laughed and giggled away. They told her she was just visions. So, Jade took her friends to the ruins to meet Savic Nano. When they got to the ruins, she began calling the ghost, but he would not appear.

I told you; I told you; it was just your imagination you see, there are no such things as ghosts. They played for a little while and went back home. Therefore, the next morning, she went back to the ruins by herself. Then, she called upon the ghost to appear.

She asked the ghost; why you didn't show yourself to my friends yesterday? When I called you. You see, I do not appear to just anybody, but you are an incredibly gifted child. Do I have special powers? Yes, of the mind.

You are a mind-reader and clairvoyant. That is why you were able to see me. How come I have not realized this on my own? You will find out in time, but right now, you are too young. For sure you will get the hang of it sooner than you think. You just got to believe. Wow, that sounds amazing!

Meanwhile, you should keep this a secret until you can dominate your gifts. Foremost, talking to Slit is a wonderful alternative!

Don't worry, it will develop bit by bit, just give it a chance. Jade was impressed that she owned these gifts which were inside of her. Time went on, and one day, she woke and found herself drifting from bed and flying around the room. It was a horrifying experience dealing with her talents for the first time.

She felt this magic was just a dream come true. Suddenly, her mother called, and she lost concentration as she landed flat on her face. What just happened? she asked. Is this normal? When she went to see Savic Nano and told him.

He grinned and said, "I told you it was going to happen. I could see it." It was her first time, but after that, she was even able to speak to Slit. As she matured, she kept her gifts as personal secrets, never sharing them with her parents. She would visit the ghost often, and he taught her how to control her powers. "Especially the powers of the mind."

As Jade matured so did her talents, perfecting them with the help of   his   friend   Savic   Nano.

Always try not to use them too often, only when necessary. Jade kept her friendship with the ghost and the serpent.

However, she moved away from the area where she used to live, and lost contact. Jade began studying at the University of Research and Mind Control. Though, she was remarkably busy and couldn't travel back-and-forth.

Unfortunately, the University was far away from her hometown. Even though, she remembered all the fun times spent with Savic Nano and Slit. Learning so much from her ghost friend was an incredible experience, which will never be forgotten.

As she grew, Jade perfected her powers. Soon she will graduate, get married, and start a family of her own. Nevertheless, Savic Nano was an incredibly good ghost and exceptional friend.

As Jade accumulated plenty of knowledge and a wonderful relationship with Savic Nano. Knowing that "not all ghosts are mean!" Hopefully, one day he will be called to finish his journey.

The angel will come for him in time. For sure she will miss his guidance very much, and the bond which grew between the "Ghost and the Serpent."

The Legend of Annabel

At times, when children would not go to sleep. The parents would scare them with the tale of "Annabel the mule without a head." However, some people believe it was just a folklore tale. To scare the tourists who drove through the town. Creating an unforgettable humorous and malicious deception.

The city dwellers have seen her trotting through the night and have heard her stumping her hooves against the barn doors, trying to find her head. The story of the mule was not a happy one.

Sadly, Annabel's head was lost during the Civil War. In one of the conflicts, a dynamite exploded extremely close and took her head off completely.No one knows why she keeps appearing as a ghost mule. Moreover, everyone around the town gets very fearful, knowing she will return.

As they suspect, she is going to come back to claim her head. The mule belonged to a farmer near the town of Manchester. When the Civil War began in 1861, they needed lots of mules to carry heavy loads of the soldiers' ammunition; rifles, dynamite, and their personal belongings.

The mules were sometimes abused by carrying extremely heavy convoys. Although, that was their job, and all the farmers had to surrender them to the army posts. Annabel's name was included in the list.

She was well-mannered and extremely intelligent. All the kids in town knew Annabel not for being stubborn. "On the contrary, she was a very smart mule." Every time she would pass by the fruit stand, she would get an apple and pear treat. Given to her by the fruit stand owner for being such a gentle mule.

"Unfortunately, that frightful day on early spring; poor Annabel lost her head." She never complained about helping the squad; she was extremely humble and nice. Foremost, she was always eager to help, bond with the soldiers, listening to their commands.

They all missed her very much when she passed away. But they believe she comes back to find her head. Especially when night falls since, that is when poor Annabel lost her head. She will keep looking for her head unstoppably. She will find it one day, and ease her pain.

Meanwhile, everyone continues to be scared when they mentioned Annabel, will come back looking around to find her head. "Or perhaps, find someone else's head." Being replaced by an overall earnestly relief. Bizarre and eerie as it might sound. Annabel deserves to finally, ease her restless desperation; which keeps haunting everyone's perception.

"The Legend of Annabel" the mule without a head, still spreads throughout the Town of Manchester.

The Stranger

Long ago, in a small town called Persimmon, children kept disappearing when walking alone at night.

Horrible stories started spreading, creating unexpected uneasiness within the town. They believed a Demon could have stolen the children or even the Witch of the forest for her black magic witchcraft. Others thought it was hungry wolves after easy prey. But no matter what, children kept missing as they never returned home.

After a while, the town began searching the grounds, and cornfields to see if they could find out what was happening, and why the children were missing? Although, when the adults began checking they could not find anything at all.

The children of the town were prohibited from walking alone late at night. Especially around the area where the young ones had vanished.

After many weeks nothing seemed out of the ordinary. Therefore, the people tried going back to their normal lives. However, they began realizing that whatever was taking the kids was extremely cunning, not showing up on the radar or triggering any of the alarms. They began doubling their efforts paying close attention during the night and watching their surroundings very carefully.

That is when things change drastically. Something or someone commenced stealing the kids from their own beds. Horrified by the terrible events, they began forming a security post all around the perimeters of the town. Never leaving the children unattended throughout the day. Steadily guarding at night to keep the children safe!

Every single sector was heavily watched during all hours. Even though, the youngsters were still being taken away. How could this be happening if we are all taking turns to gape at the protected perimeters? But we have not been able to see anything come in or out.

The townspeople were astonished by what was going on. So finally, they called Sheriff Bronson from the closest town and explained the whole situation. They agreed with each other that they required more manpower to finally, find a way to end this bizarre tragedy.

However, he knew of a task force he had befriended and was going to let them know. Soon after, other children were taken away in the same exact way.

After two whole days, they saw a team of soldiers appear in the distance. Upon arrival they disclosed that Sheriff Bronson had contacted them to help with the search.

The town had many forests and mountains that anyone could hide. The team told the town citizens they would scour the area up and down. They were confident that they would find their children.

Searching many miles all through the day, they did not find a single clue. They felt confused and puzzled, not being able to find whom or what was taking the town's children. Searching through the forest, corn fields, and other places as they were targeting very dangerous terrain, without finding out anything or having a shred of evidence. They could not imagine who was doing this.

After daybreak, they head back to town, confused that after searching the vast forests and mountains, they had found nothing remotely close to animal or human footprints were not discovered. The people became shocked at their conclusion and needed to find a way of getting the crisis resolved.

The soldier's squad gave the townspeople the telephone number of an office that investigated "unsolved mysteries." With no time to lose, they contacted the phone number, and a lady answered and told them they were quite busy and did not have time to waste. They assured the lady their story was true and were desperate to find the missing children.

The investigative team showed up at the town and they asked to describe in detail when and where these disappearances took place. The town was concerned because they were afraid to lose more of their youngsters. The parents could not sleep, paying close attention to their loved ones.

The lady and her team introduced themselves and told the town to be on full alert. Anything suspicious was to be reported at once. The lady said you can call me Sandy. My team is composed of two other partners, Benjamin, and Dann. We are here to get answers to this strange, unexplained occurrence.

They set up all their equipment and began watching their screens very closely. After about three hours of surveillance, some movement appeared which could not be corroborated.

No one was carrying the child. However, it was floating through the air, completely asleep.

The camera could not pick up any other image or how the child was being suspended.

Sandy ran outside and tried to pick up the child with her hands, stopping her from floating, but a magnetic field was making it hard for her to do so. She then followed the child's body without making a sound.

Finally, she saw what she feared the most, a Sphere floating in place. As the door opened widely, the child was placed in a clear tube. I realized we were dealing with something from out of space.

Suddenly, a creature crawled out of a chamber and did not look very social. It tried to bite me on the hand, as I began hitting it with the back of my gun. Struggling to subdue the creature, I ended up pushing it toward the chamber with all my strength. I couldn't climb back in and close the door, because the lock was jammed.

I continued investigating inside the Sphere, but very cautiously. Most definitely, it was not like the ET movie. They were hostile.

As I began walking through the Sphere, everything looked very sophisticated and beyond my comprehension.

I found more hanging tubes inside as other children were wearing oxygen masks and completely asleep. It was a frightful scene, and I needed to find a lever or handle to open the tubes and free them all.

After many minutes had passed, I could not find any way to open the tubes.I communicated with my partners to rush over to help me out. I felt a tentacle on the side of my neck trying to strangle me. I tried to move to the other side, but the creature tossed me across the Sphere violently.

After hitting my head, I stood up, and he wanted to pick me up again. Somehow, I ran to the other room to stay clear of this aggressive beast. It was a huge monster with claws and sharp tentacles ready to strike.

The monster was enraged, stopping my efforts to release the children. Doing everything possible to stop us! In his second assault, my team was there already helping me find a way to free the kids and struggling with the monster.

We were trying to force the door to open; alongside the long hallway. Evading the creature which looked overly powerful. Besides, it could not understand anything we were saying. I was checking out all the maneuvers to open the tubes. But despite my efforts, I did not know how to get them to open.

Benjamin walked to the other side of the aisle and was able to see a handle which was kept in a locked room. We were trying to force the door to open, alongside the long corridor and get access to the leverage.

After wrestling for a bit, we pulled the handle down and the tubes lifted upward. Consequently, Dann was waiting on the other side. He was able to take the children out. We kept the monster far away from the kids aiming to restrain him as much as we could. We did not want to shoot inside the Sphere since the bullets could bounce and ricochet in other directions and hurt the children and us in the process.

For a moment, we thought we had everything under control, but the monster kept fighting to escape our grasp and keep the children in the tubes. We realized we could not communicate with the creature at all. It was an extremely savage beast without any social skills.

He just wanted the children to perform experiments on them. Nonetheless, building a large group to take them away forever.

Through all this, Benjamin had called the town residents to help defeat   the   monster. They came with all sorts of shovels, iron bars, pics, anything they could find. As they all entered the Sphere and confronted the monster.

The team effort paid off, and finally, they defeated the creature. We were able to free the children at last! We thought of burning the Sphere to destroy the monster. Taking precautions so it would not try to steal any other child. We knew by destroying it. The town would finally gain some peace of mind. Subsequently, the town was yearning to put an end to this tragic situation.

However, as we got prepared to exterminate the Sphere, we heard it turn on. Disappearing in thin air like it was never there. The townspeople did not know how to thank us for returning their children unharmed. In appreciation, they prepared a huge food festival in our honor to show their gratitude.

The morning after, we got ready to load the equipment in our jeep.

We had to head back to the city. More unsolved cases were pending for us to investigate.

Sandy was glad to resolve another case. Benjamin and Dann were hopeful that they would continue to unravel the unknown which exists all around us.

As sometimes, we are too busy to realize the mysteries which lay dormant to be discovered.

Thriller

Black Shadows

Knowing time changes like the wind.

I still remember the day when I felt empty.

Believing that life is not always the same.

The weakness of one's soul becomes a target.

Friends pretending, they are by your side.

"Those who seek to destroy us with envy and goulash thoughts."

They are satisfied by our desperation.

Certainly, we are on the brink of loneliness.

They engorge themselves when we are down in the gutter

with no escape but the will to survive!

Making it possible for black shadows to embellish our existence.

After all, they are imperfect souls flourishing through

the pain of others.

Even though, they cannot find happiness within their lives, they

find ways to hurt us.

"Walking on this earth trying to destroy all that is good with

their evil selfishness."

Imposters of good faith pretending to be our friend.

Making false statements and compromising the overall standards

with their wickedness.

"Betrayals of humanity dwelling in the black shadows of

everlasting dismay."

Green Creeper

In the dark coldness of my room, I laid down in bed
and fell asleep.
As the night lingered on, my heart awoke with thumping sounds.
I saw myself in a nearby graveyard as
I tried to run away; I was stuck in a deep hole of no return.
My feet and hands were bound together.
I wanted to open my eyes.
However, they had been threaded with fishing twine.
Struggling to catch my breath, I found no air.
I was trapped in this evil circumstance without a way out forever.
I screamed! As loud as I could, but no one heard
my terrifying shouts!
Suddenly, a moving sound shocked me, without a doubt.
A ghost appeared in front of me, all green with bright red eyes.
A hideous creature that was not going to let me survive.
He began smothering my airways. I almost passed out.
His black shadow hung over me
as piercing daggers burned my flesh deep into my skin.
I was terrified and overpowered by this
frightful presence next to me.
I felt chills down my spine and ready to take my last breath.
Why couldn't I break free?

Asking myself how can I get rid of this creepy, eerie thing?

My horror was intense as the Green Creeper

dragged me closer to him.

Getting on top of my body and with his serpent twirled tonged,

using it to slurp-up my soul onto his wet, slimy mouth.

I am fighting with this sinister demon, pushing, and shoving

away.

Somehow, being under pressure, I do not know where I

found the strength.

A grotesque and tenebrous ghost searching for victims at night.

Using bodies until they are burned and dry.

A gruesome, ugly creature with a devouring appetite.

I am in a dire situation with no escape from the jaws of Hell.

This disturbing apparition kidnapped my every dream.

"Utterly ravishing my domain."

Taking over my skeleton and bones to fulfill his macabre plan.

Though, my will to live kicked in,

and I changed his maleficent program.

He is a villain in disguise! Going after your soul and pride.

After what I endured, my self-preservation kept me alive.

"Instinctively, I fought back!"

Furthermore, he choked and assaulted me when I was

most vulnerable.

"Wicked and vile of little worth and value."

No matter how much I pleaded, he tried to steal my soul.

In the gloomy night, I saw a light pouring down like rain.

"The Prince of Power pulled me up and saved my life

from the damnation of Hell."

Beware of his existence changes in deceptive ways

traps you in his web of lies and carries you away.

Moreover, I am not his only victim.

He will continue to seek other souls;

uses our dreams as an opened door to destroy our existence.

Eventually, I was hovering over a blue and golden sky,

I was able to return to my body by the wings of angels.

"At last, I was at peace and free!"

The Green Creeper stays in the black hole of our dreams.

Waiting for opportunities to steal the very

essence of our emotions.

"He is a cowardly, ghoulish ghost going after

our spirit and soul."

To satisfy his bizarre hunger and degradation.

Halloween

Ghosts and Goblins are lurking away
we are getting closer to Halloween Day.
Witches and brooms are ready to fly
looking for kids to snatch through the night.
No one escapes the horror of sounds.
Werewolves are howling all over the town.
Vampires are hungry, they will clinch at your neck.
Watch out for the Zombies as they step on your head.
Mummies get ready to wrap you in cloth
do not look at their eyes, they will curse you with dust.
Scary bugs are lighting the way
bats on a mission to feed on your blood instead.
Spirits appeared in the dark narrow streets.
Skeletons are dancing and "Jack-O-Lanterns" are lit.
Children dressed-up for the occasion
knocking on doors and screaming!
"Trick or Treat!" Give me something good to eat
is the 'Halloween' celebration.
Pointing to their flashlights as they walk down the block.
For chocolates, caramel apples, and candy rock.
The fog is dense, something is grabbing at your feet.
Running away is a sensible thing.

Fear is felt everywhere!

Not to mention, it feels neat I could swear.

The black family cat storms out like a flash!

"Hocus-pocus" 12:00 o'clock; October 31ˢᵗ, as we celebrate.

"Halloween Day" the perfect Holiday blast!

Living with the Enemy

It's hard, too hard to cope, trying to compromise with emptiness.

Foremost, knowing it could change in a split second

blindsided by pain.

Living with a dark soul enemy

destroying everything you've built for so long.

Finding no options or change

always thirsty for power, greed, and control.

Watching with vengeance to feed his malicious epitome.

Therefore, I keep strolling away, walking down on eggshells

unforgiving humiliation and pretense.

Going after a break but disturbed voices

filled with unruly anger lingers in place.

Despite good attributes, every sound seems to ripped the heart

apart without any concern.

However, final actions are up for grabs.

The preparation stalks the brain and, like a storm of vengeance

tearing down everything planted in the rain.

Shredding the deep end of one's moral

tossed like garbage through the air.

Limitless, to regain confidence, praying for inner peace

but not there.

Don't care about feelings; irrational tantrums are displayed.

Nothing matters. His selfish ego takes center stage.

For that reason, he shows his true colors of wicked evilness.

Malevolent conflicts, losing everything you've cared for,

all taken away.

Left with a broken memory that won't heal around this madness!

It takes a mind of his own as a dark entity surrounds him.

Deceitful rage begins to appear; nonetheless,

vicious actions reveal deviance from the unknown.

Vindictive behavior opened scars dried-up in the sun.

Bending to "pick up the pace."

However, the horizon seems bleak.

Screaming! For justice, besides, no one listened to my plea.

But reckoning is a step away!

As demon powers destroy people's dreams.

In this treacherous ride, I am left with total grief.

Walking toward a better tomorrow, trusting,

"God is my witness."

The "Holy Father" who will never abandon me.

Mysterious Goblins

Besides being born different, a dwarf with hideous pointed ears,

rough skin, which clouds their face like brown bark from a tree.

Making their race hard to survive, most definitely.

Hiding in dark caves, trying to remain unexposed.

Staying away from the naked eye is the perfect stroll.

Shielding from sunlight in deep caves, they rest.

Avoiding the presence of strangers, they want to forget!

Sharp teeth like needles, sagging skin wrapped in wolf's hair.

Surviving every day requires lots of planning and tedious work.

Hoods covering their heads while dressed in transparent suede.

Armed and ready to fight for their home and domain.

Humming softly through the vast forest of deep evergreen plains.

Although they are ugly creatures.

Still, fearless to the end.

Goblin society is known to hide from those who do not

understand their ways.

From emeralds to diamonds in the rough.

Goblins are the "creators of gemstones"

kept hidden in deep chambers

secretly buried through time.

Many hidden treasures of the most brilliant precious stones.

Furthermore, there are quite many and, at times, children

glance a peek at who they are;

of course, being different from the rest.

Their innocence is the clue which enables the Goblins to modify

their behavior.

Besides being ugly little creatures hiding in the dark

with yellow eyes which light in the darkness of the night.

"Making themselves visible to whomever wins their heart."

Red Moon

Flying high in the sky, angry birds of prey are

secretly hiding in the Mountain of Flames.

Demonic dark powers often are felt.

It is said it holds the beginning and the end.

"The red moon sparks the dominion where evil dwells."

As it carries the echoing voices of Hell.

Although, its strength comes when the fire turns into flames.

It begins when the soil becomes unstable and disturbed.

The fury of the wind brings thunder on his way.

Melting the trees that grow by the rocky terrain.

Between the gassy smells of Sulphur which linger on its wake.

The smoke becomes dense as the fog begins to fade.

The red moon proceeds closely and attracts some of the heat.

"Then turns into shadows with each bewildering plea."

The silence of the night waits for the bewitching hour to strike.

The red moon smiles at the sun when her brightness spikes.

Nevertheless, rain falls controlling its temperament and rage.

All that stands around becomes blistering red.

Betrayed and angry as she begins to pose a threat.

My only hope is for "Mother Nature" to calm her

frenzy rampage.

www.ingramcontent.com/pod-product-compliance
Lightning Source LLC
Chambersburg PA
CBHW070748160726
48004CB00001B/96